Edward Bellamy

Twayne's United States Authors Series

David J. Nordloh, Editor

Indiana University, Bloomington

TUSAS 500

EDWARD BELLAMY
(1850-1898)

Edward Bellamy

By Sylvia E. Bowman

Indiana University

Twayne Publishers • *Boston*

Edward Bellamy

Sylvia E. Bowman

Copyright © 1986 by G.K. Hall & Co.
All Rights Reserved
Published by Twayne Publishers
A Division of G.K. Hall & Co.
70 Lincoln Street
Boston, Massachusetts 02111

Copyediting supervised by Lewis DeSimone
Book production by Elizabeth Todesco
Book design by Barbara Anderson

Typeset in 11 pt. Garamond
by Modern Graphics, Inc., Weymouth, Massachusetts

Printed on permanent/durable acid-free paper
and bound in the United States of America

Library of Congress Cataloging in Publication Data

Bowman, Sylvia E.
    Edward Bellamy.

   (Twayne's United States authors series; TUSAS 500)
   Bibliography: p. 151
   Includes index.
   1. Bellamy, Edward, 1850–1898—Criticism and
interpretation.   I. Title.   II. Series.
PS1087.B58   1986   813'.4   86–242
ISBN 0–8057–7460–2

Contents

About the Author

Sylvia E. Bowman, since 1980 professor emeritus of Indiana University at Fort Wayne, joined that faculty in 1947 as head of the English department, and later served as acting chairman when she was appointed chairman of arts and sciences. Later she became chancellor of the six Indiana University regional campuses—the first woman to hold such rank among the Big Ten universities.

Dr. Bowman did her undergraduate work with majors in English and history at Blackburn College, and completed it at Central Normal College in 1939; she earned her master of arts degree in English studies from the University of Chicago in 1943.

Her initial research on Bellamy was conducted as a graduate student at the Sorbonne during a three-year leave from Indiana University. There she used Bellamy's ideas as the basis for a comparative study of utopian and socioeconomic writers of Europe and America. The result was an 819-page doctoral thesis in French, which, along with two other theses related to literature, led to her receiving the doctoral degree with the very highest honors.

Her first book, *The Year 2000: A Critical Biography of Edward Bellamy*, was published in 1958; her second, prepared with the cooperation of scholars in Europe, Asia, and elsewhere, was *Edward Bellamy Abroad: An American Prophet's Influence* (1962).

Dr. Bowman has also published articles in *Etudes Anglaise, New England Quarterly, Southern Humanities Review,* and *American Literary Realism,* as well as countless book reviews. A public speaker, she was elected many years ago to the International Platform Association founded by Daniel Webster. Among other awards, she has received the Frederic Bachman Lieber Memorial Award for Distinguished Teaching (1962); the Senior Class Award for Distinguished Teaching, Indiana University, Fort Wayne (1969); the Honorary Doctor of Letters from St. Mary's College, Notre Dame, Indiana (1972); the Professional Achievement Award of the University of Chicago Alumni Association (1973); and the Helen Keller Honorary Doctorate of Humane Letters from Urbana College (1981). In May 1986, she was awarded the honorary degree of Doctor of Humane Letters by Indiana University.

Dr. Bowman founded and personally edited for eighteen years Twayne's United States Authors Series and Twayne's English Authors Series, as well as serving as general editor of Twayne's World Authors Series and Masterworks of American Literature.

Preface

Edward Bellamy's *Looking Backward* (1888) has been considered one of the most influential books published in the nineteenth century. It is republished frequently, and is still read and studied. As a result of its stimulation of thought in the late 1880s and 1890s, Bellamy clubs, better known as Nationalist clubs, were founded in many sections of the United States. Bellamy's ideas influenced not only society at large but also such important individuals as William Dean Howells, Upton Sinclair, Eugene Debs, Norman Thomas, and members of the New Deal. Because of Bellamy's Nationalism—an Americanized socialism—and his effective presentation of his future society, his views appealed more to Americans than did those of Karl Marx. In fact, the Marxists admitted that his influence helped to defeat theirs in the United States even during the crucial 1930s.

In this analytical study of Bellamy chapter 1 presents his family background and small-town environment, his religious experience and his own religion of solidarity, his independent study program, his sojourn in Germany as a student, and his study and short practice of law. It describes his career in journalism as an editorialist and a book reviewer, experiences that contributed greatly to his intellectual development and to his knowledge of the socioeconomic situation. It also surveys the lyceum talks that paved the way for the much later revelation of his Socialist thinking. Chapter 1 is also concerned with Bellamy's novels. It mentions his short stories only when they are relevant to the ideas he expressed in his other writings. (However, these short stories are listed in the Chronology in order to indicate not only his literary endeavors but his development as a writer.)

In chapter 2 the principles that Bellamy expressed in his utopian fiction and in the *New Nation* are presented; and, where space permits, his concepts are correlated with those he expressed in his editorials and book reviews in the *Springfield Union* in the 1870s. Chapter 3 identifies Bellamy's plans for the achievement of the ideal state, their method of implementation, and the functions of government. Chapter 4 is devoted to the presentation of the socioeconomic and intellectual life of the populace of the year 2000, as well as to some of the innovations Bellamy introduced. Chapter 5 discusses the influence of *Looking Backward* upon the Nationalists, the People's Party, the Theosophists, the Christian Socialists, and, last but not least, upon Norman Thomas, Eugene Debs, the New Dealers, and other important figures of the twentieth century. Unfortunately, space does not permit full discussion of Bellamy's influence on such literary personalities as William Dean Howells, Ignatius Donnelly, and Albion Tourgee, or of the spate of pro- and anti-utopian novels which answered his.

In fact, this final chapter merely opens the door for future research and for a study of Bellamy's influence upon religious leaders, the Socialists, the Progressives, the New Dealers, and American literary figures. Such detailed research needs to be done not only because of the role Bellamy's thinking played in the past but because of the solutions he might provide to the society of the 1980s. As we face the problems of the postindustrial era, it is merely wisdom to review the past to locate possible solutions.

Because of the significance of Bellamy's ideas, they have been given priority over everything else; as a result, the material in the Bibliography has been limited to essential publications, and the articles referred to in Notes and References are not repeated in the Bibliography.

The Bellamy manuscripts deposited in the Houghton Library, Harvard University, and his published works are quoted with the written permission of the late Paul Bellamy; his sister, the late Marion Earnshaw Bellamy; and their mother, the late Emma Bellamy.

Sylvia E. Bowman

Indiana University

Chronology

1850   Edward Bellamy born, 26 March, to Rev. Rufus King and Maria Putnam Bellamy in Chicopee Falls, Massachusetts.

1864   After a profound religious experience, Edward is baptized on 13 April.

1867   Fails to pass physical examination for West Point; becomes independent reader and student at Union College, Schenectady, New York. Interested in Comte and Socialism.

1868–1869   With his cousin, William Packer, lives and studies in Germany.

1868   Begins study of law in Springfield, Massachusetts.

1871   Passes bar examination with distinction; opens law office in Chicopee Falls and closes it after one case. Publishes "Woman Suffrage" in *Golden Age*.

1872   To New York City to be free-lance journalist. Publishes "Railroad Disasters" and "National Education" in *Golden Age*.

1872–1877   Works for the *Springfield Union* as editorial writer and book reviewer; presents two lyceum speeches containing basic concepts later used in *Looking Backward*.

1873   Writes "Religion of Solidarity," his basic lifelong belief.

1875   First short story, "The Cold Snap" (September).

1876   "A Providence" and "The Old Folks' Party" (stories).

1877   "Lost," "A Summer Evening's Dream," "Taking a Mean Advantage," "Superfluity of Naughtiness," "A Mid-Night Dream," "Hooking Watermelons," and "Extra Hazardous" (stories).

1877–1878   Leaves *Springfield Union;* tours Hawaiian Islands and elsewhere with brother Frederick.

1878   "Two Days' Solitary Imprisonment," "Pott's Painless

Cure," "Deserted" (stories). First novel: *Six to One: A Nantucket Idyl.*

1878–1879   *Dr. Heidenhoff's Process* serialized in *Springfield Union;* published as book in 1880.

1879   Stories "Jane Hicks" and "Taking a Mean Advantage"; novel *The Duke of Stockbridge* serialized in *Berkshire Courier.*

1880   Charles and Edward Bellamy found the *Penny News* in Springfield (February); by 13 May, it becomes the *Daily News.* "That Letter" and "A Tale of the South Pacific."

1882   Marries Emma Sanderson, 30 May.

1884   Son Paul born, 26 December; Edward retires from economically troubled *Daily News* to write fiction. *Miss Ludington's Sister,* serialized in *Literary World* and published as a book.

1886   Daughter Marion born, 4 March. "The Blindman's World" and "Echo of Antietam."

1887   "At Pinney's Ranch." First edition of *Looking Backward.*

1888   Revised edition of *Looking Backward.* "A Love Story Reversed."

1889   First meeting of the Boston Bellamy Club 8 January; February, club decides to publish the monthly magazine the *Nationalist;* "To Whom This May Come" and "A Positive Romance."

1891   Bellamy founds the *New Nation,* 31 January. The *Nationalist* ceases publication with March-April issue.

1891–1894   Bellamy and Nationalists deeply involved with Populism; Bellamy ceases publication of the *New Nation,* 1894.

1897   *Equality* published. Bellamy and his family leave in the fall to reside in Denver because of his ill health.

1898   Returns to Chicopee Falls. Dies, 22 May. *The Blindman's World and Other Stories.*

1900   *The Duke of Stockbridge.*

1972   The Bellamy House on 191 Church Street declared a national landmark in June by the National Park Service.

1973   The Edward Bellamy Memorial Association buys the Bellamy House.

1974   Restoration of the Bellamy House undertaken with the aid of the Society for the Preservation of New England Antiquity. A bibliography, "The Bellamy Collection of Memorabilia," compiled by Mark S. and Stephen R. Jendrysik for the Bellamy Association.

Chapter One
Religion, Rebellion, Solution, and Fiction

Chicopee Falls, Massachusetts, where Edward Bellamy was born before the Civil War and where he lived after it, was an industrial town. The Connecticut River had been harnessed soon after a settlement was made there to provide power for the saw and grist mills. By 1810, when the first cotton mill was established, the history of Chicopee's industries had begun; by the late 1880s, the cotton mills employed more people than any other industry; but the town was also famous for the swords, bayonets, and cannon produced by the Ames Manufacturing Company, for the bicycles of the Overman Wheel Company, and for its knitting machines, sportsman's rifles, and agricultural implements.[1]

The parents of Edward Bellamy, the Reverend Rufus King Bellamy and Maria Putnam Bellamy, the daughter of the Reverend Benjamin Putnam of Springfield, Massachusetts, lived in a two-story house that was not far from the beautiful river, the cotton mills, and the row upon row of stark, unattractive, yardless brick tenement houses, called "huddles," in which the factory workers lived. Near the Bellamy residence were the large homes of the factory owners and agents whom Bellamy described in a journal as those who molded the destiny of the people, controlled the churches by hiring and firing the ministers, and determined the nature of every social and public enterprise. To Bellamy, these managers were to be compared "to the feudal baron dwelling among the people. There is undoubtedly no sort of human greatness so solidly satisfying as that of a local magnate. Let Napoleon and Alexander sigh for worlds to conquer. The man who rules his village is a more complete rogue than they."[2]

Unlike Napoleon, who did not dwell with all those he injured, the factory agent lived among the laborers; and, like Bellamy, he saw the bedraggled, stunted children who worked in the mills. Unlike the agent, Bellamy's compassion was aroused; and he was

1

indignant about a civilization that would so sacrifice "human rights and well-being."[3] Like Charles Kingsley, Bellamy could have written that "From my cradle, as the son of an active clergyman, I have been brought up in the most familiar intercourse with the poor in town and country."[4]

The Religious Family

Bellamy's parents were the descendants of old New England families; and their ancestors, who had settled in the colonies in the 1630s and 1640s, had been merchants, schoolmasters, and ministers. The most famous of these ancestors was Rufus Bellamy's great-grandfather, the Reverend Joseph Bellamy, who worked closely with Jonathan Edwards in the Great Awakening and who preached in his sermon of 13 May 1762 that "Love is radically the whole of that duty which God requires of man." To Joseph Bellamy, as to Edward, brotherly love would be the end of "malice and envy" and of "tattling and backbiting," for "undissembled love and good will" would reign.[5]

Like that famous ancestor, the Reverend Rufus Bellamy, Bellamy's father, a stocky, portly Baptist, "was known and honored all over Western Massachusetts, and especially loved for his quiet and modest ways of 'going about doing good' among the people of his charge."[6] Incapable of condemning his fellowmen in words and of not finding some good in them, Rufus Bellamy was theologically ahead of his time because he could not subscribe to the theory of eternal damnation; and he expressed from his pulpit doubts about the existence of hell.[7] The Reverend Bellamy was friendly to all he met, and he was famous for his keen wit, his intelligence, his yarn-spinning skill, and his prayers—which were deemed better than his long sermons.[8]

Although Maria Putnam Bellamy was, like her beloved and sympathetic husband, a dominating personality, she possessed more of the stiff, unbending qualities of the early Puritans. Cold, reserved, and intelligent, she had a keen, New England sense of duty; and she too was so kind to her fellowmen that she was constantly carrying a bowl of broth, fresh eggs, or jelly to someone ill or in need— and whether the person she helped was a Catholic or a Baptist did not matter.[9] According to Mason Green, a friend of and co-worker with Edward Bellamy and author of an unpublished biography of him, Mrs. Bellamy's "chief consideration," after "revealed religion," was a "high aim in life. . . . She regarded the main purpose of life to be discipline of the heart, soul, and mind, and deprivation of sense gratifications she regarded not as a misfortune but as a blessing and benefit. The unwritten law of the house was that the boys should not waste their time."[10]

Mrs. Bellamy, whose father, the Reverend Benjamin Putnam, believed in the equal education of women, had been so well educated that she read Greek and Latin.[11] She delighted in teaching and study.[12] As her son Frederick recalled, his mother's command, whenever one of her sons was idle, was "get a book," and she meant an informative book. Novels seemed to her to be useless material; and the newspapers, which Rufus Bellamy encouraged the boys to read, were not so important as histories to their mother.[13] As might be expected, the parents and their four sons—Packer, Frederick, Edward, and Charles—had long discussions about serious problems. Edward, who did not participate like the others, most enjoyed private conversations with his brother Charles, who was also to write serious and utopian novels,[14] and with his mother. After the death of Packer, the mother's favorite son, Edward was selected to take his place in her heart and mind; he seems to have had better rapport with her than with anyone else.[15]

The Bellamy family shared not only an intellectual life but, as might be expected, a deeply religious one; family prayers were said once or twice each day, each child had his own prayers, and on Sundays the children attended not only Sunday School but two other services.[16] Edward became the cause of special prayers by the family; for, when he reached the age of discretion, he had not yet had a religious experience. Finally, however, at fourteen he had a coming of the light, and was baptized on 13 April 1864. He wrote many years later, in his unfinished autobiography, about the effect of his Calvinistic indoctrination and of his recognition of himself as an abject sinner who had to make his peace with God or suffer terrible consequences:[17]

Accordingly he submitted to the emotional experience of a religious conversion. He came to feel a sense of intimacy and to enjoy an indescribably close and tender communion with what seemed to him a very real and sublime being. . . . In prayer he took a deep and awful pleasure; it was to him a sensation at once of almost sensuous happiness as of ineffable sublimity when at such times his heart seemed to throb with that of duty and his soul seemed fused and melted in perfect unison with the divine. A love more tender and passionate than any with which human charms ever moved him seemed to bind him. . . . to the infinite. . . . He saw the world with new eyes. [18]

During this emotional experience, when "there were always two to consult on every step, himself and his deity," [19] Bellamy delved so deeply into religious literature and so studied the Bible that he knew it thoroughly. He later won a biblical quotation game with missionaries while on board a ship to the Sandwich Islands. [20] He frequently quoted the Bible in his written work and successfully imitated biblical style in the "Parable of the Water Tank" in *Equality*.

Despite his religious preoccupations and reading, Bellamy and his brothers had, as boys, their "share of toys and marbles, fights and kites" [21]; and, as young men, they indulged in drinking and "were considered rather high living young men by the godly folk of the village." [22] Close in their family ties and associations, the Bellamy children and their parents formulated a home life that, as Edward admitted, bound people to persons rather than places. To him, the love of home "is one of the strongest, the purest, the most unselfish passions that human nature knows." [23] And, as he revealed in one of his journals, Bellamy had a "deep-seated aversion to change"; [24] he never truly left his home in Chicopee, despite his sojourns away from it.

Before young Edward completed his secondary education, he wrote essays indicating his interest in heroes: "Philip and Alexander," "The Marshalls of Napoleon," and "Notes on Military Tactics." As these compositions indicate, he was interested in a military career. When he could not pass his physical examination in 1867 for entrance to West Point, his career changed; but his interest in military tactics was never lost, despite his hatred of war. [26] To his mother, the continued education of Edward was a problem; for she thought him "too young, especially not being stronger, to enter college next fall, and doubtless there are ways in which his time can be spent profitably." As she noted, "The only difficulty is to know what to do with him *in school* in the interval. He has read nearly all the Latin and Greek, and been over more than all in Algebra and Geometry that they do the senior year in Easthampton or other preparatory school." [27]

When Frederick Bellamy returned to Union College, Schenectady, New York, in the fall of 1867, Edward, now seventeen, accompanied him as an independent student who had his own educational program. In October Edward wrote "Necessary Self Education," an inventory of his studies; he recorded a "thorough acquaintance with history of the world, Social and Political, ancient and modern," as well as with "Physical and Political Geography"; "the Laws of Society in its life and government, which Laws are properly comprehended in the subject of Political Economy"; "French and Spanish Languages . . . with other of the principal modern languages as may be attainable without the neglect of other branches of study"; and "theory of Military science."

He also listed items to be studied: "works of mental science and logical demonstration . . . to strengthen and methodize the operations of the mind"; "public speaking and writing"; "such moral self-education as shall prevent me from yielding or departing from my high purpose through any temptation of personal reputation or indolent repose, or any other influence whatsoever." And he goes on, interestingly, "Finally, in addition to this system of study, such requirements of general knowledge, of mental discipline, of conversational power, of acquaintance with human nature as developed in myself and in others, by introspection and extrospection, as may altogether make up the accomplishments of those purposes in life to which I have appointed myself." Last and least he refers to "the physical system." Since his mother had suffered from tuberculosis when she married and since Packer and Edward both were to die of it, Bellamy should have been more concerned about his physical welfare than he suggests in referring to "such care and strengthening and discipline as shall prepare it to be the effective instrument of my mind through life."[28]

Very little has been recorded about the year Bellamy spent at Union College, but he wrote in a journal that he was to be more a "reader rather than a student, devoting much more attention to the college library than to the college textbooks."[29] As Frederick Bellamy made clear many years later, Edward prevailed upon one of the professors to give him a special course in literature;[30] and, as other records indicate, he joined the fraternity Alpha Kappa Epsilon and the Philomathean Society.[31] Although Bellamy's intellectual experience at Union College is somewhat of a blank, comments in his fiction reflect some of his views and attitudes. Although Frederick indicated that Edward was a recluse, it is more likely that Edward—if he did indeed fill his fiction with details of his own experience—enjoyed what he depicts in "Pott's Painless Cure" (1879): conversations with other college boys about ideas. Moreover, his reaction to the rigid religious intolerance of the college[32] is contained in "A Positive Romance," which describes the central character's indoctrination with Auguste Comte's Positivism while he is attending a college that "was a little one-horse institution, but blue as a whetstone in its orthodoxy; and with my father, who was a clergyman of a very strict sect and staid views, that fact covered a multitude of shortcomings."[33] The name of Comte was marked out in the existing manuscript, but was not deleted when the story was printed. The manuscript reference could mean that Bellamy had become acquainted with the Frenchman's ideas and also with those of the Socialists during his stay at Union College. After *Looking Backward* appeared, his Union College contemporary Isaac Landt, an attorney and a Populist, wrote Bellamy that he had read the novel and that he had "then thought it was a production just like you and wonder if it could be Ed. of Old Union."[34]

If the religious, economic, or political concepts Edward Bellamy generated or was exposed to while attending Union College are unrecoverable, there is no more certainty about what his 1868–1869 sojourn in Europe gave him. During his reading period at Union College Edward's brother Packer, who was traveling with his cousin William Packer in Europe, died; and Edward, because his mother insisted that he "make the sacrifice" and forget his "selfish pride," reluctantly went with William to Dresden, Germany, where the cousin's mother, Mrs. Harriet Packer, installed them in a German home. The young cousins learned to read and write German, but very little is known about what they actually studied, or about what lectures they attended. Although Edward's brother Frederick recalled in 1916 that his brother's letters to him from Germany were full of German socialism, he added that Edward had "read and studied [it] much at home."[35]

In 1894, in an article in the *Ladies' Home Journal,* Bellamy recounted "how much more deeply that [European] black background of misery impressed me than the palaces and cathedrals." According to this article, Bellamy and William Packer discussed "finding some great remedy for poverty, some plan for equalizing human conditions. Our discussions usually brought up against the same old

stump: who would do the dirty work? We did not realize, as probably few do who lightly dismiss the subject of social reform with
the same query, that its logic implies the condonation of all forms
of slavery. Not until we all acknowledge the world's 'dirty work'
as our common and equal responsibility, shall we be in a position
intelligently to consider, or have the disposition seriously to seek,
a just and reasonable way of distributing and adjusting the burden."[36]
After his return to the United States, Bellamy began the study
of law in the office of Leonard and Wells in Springfield, Massachusetts;[37] and he recorded in one of his Eliot Carson notebooks, which
contain materials that parallel his life and thought, his reasons, aside
from those stated in "Necessary Self-Education," for preparing to
be a lawyer: "What he had had in his mind's eye when taking to
the law, was the arguing of great constitutional questions, the
chivalrous defense of the widow and the orphan against oppressors,
and the vindication of accused and sorely beset innocence."[38] Bellamy passed the bar examinations with such brilliance in 1871 that
M. B. Whitney, a Westfield lawyer of repute, offered him a partnership in his firm; Bellamy chose, however, to open his own office
in Chicopee. But, when his first and only case involved evicting a
widow for nonpayment of rent, he became disgusted with the trade
of being a "public blood hound" and removed his shingle.[39] As a
result of his experience, Bellamy was to criticize the legal profession
in his editorials and novels as the upholder of plutocracy: still, his
training was invaluable not only to his logical thinking but also to
the knowledge of law and government that were so important to
his depiction of his ideal state. As Bellamy himself observed some
years later, "unless a man knows something about law. . . . as to
how the world has been and is governed, he's unlikely to be a sound
adviser as to how the present methods can be improved on. The
man who undertakes to mend a machine must understand it as it
was made."[40]
After his venture with the practice of law, another valuable development occurred: he began his literary career and the practice of
writing for newspapers which was to occupy him intermittently
throughout his life and which was to be another phase of the education of the reformer. In March 1871 while still in Chicopee,
Bellamy published in the *Golden Age,* a radical weekly edited by
Theodore Tilton, one of his first known articles—"Woman Suffrage."[41] In September 1871 William Packer wrote to Bellamy to

inform him that he had applied for Edward for a "literary situation" with Carleton L. Lewis, managing editor of the New York *Evening Post* and a friend of the Packers. When William had told Lewis about Edward's article in the *Golden Age* and had also referred the editor to Thomas W. Higginson for more information about his cousin, Lewis asked William if Edward was capable of writing about home politics, as well as about other subjects of current interest, and requested that Edward submit to him a sample editorial.[42] As a result of William's interest and of the work he submitted to Lewis, Edward Bellamy went to New York to live. Rather than living with the wealthy Packer family, he took rooms for himself in Stuyvesant Square.[43] Although he must have contributed articles whenever he could, none of them has been located. He did contribute in March 1872 two articles to the *Golden Age:* "Railroad Disasters" and "National Education."[44] In a note in his journal for a sequel to *Looking Backward,* Bellamy was probably recalling his own experience in New York: "hard to live. Sees lots of suffering, becomes a Nationalist."[45]

Rebellion

Bellamy's experience in New York ended when he returned to Chicopee Falls after a letter in May 1872 from his father informed him that some of the staff of the *Springfield Republican* had purchased the *Union.* Wrote the Reverend Bellamy, "It struck me that possibly if you were on the ground at this crisis you *might* get your foot in— I don't know as it would suit your ideas, or your *politics,* if you have any just at this time. But as the two papers take opposite sides you might pay your money and take your choice."[46]

Bellamy worked for the *Union* from 1872 to 1877 as an editorial writer and book reviewer. More important as sources of information about his personal views, he presented two lyceum speeches during that period.

In his first lyceum address he foresaw the day when the power of the people would lead to their full domination; and he announced that that "great day" was one "toward whose bright dawning the ages have travailed together in anguish." The process that would dissolve "the twin tyrannies of ignorance and political oppression" was to be peaceful and would be the result of the education and the decision of the people, not that of the demagogues.[47] In his second lyceum talk Bellamy discussed the tyranny of wealth, wage slavery, and the necessity of work; and he denounced the industrial system as "social barbarism" and as a "system which shamed humanity before God and the angels." After stating that the industrial system was inconsistent with the "plainest principles of equity" and was "founded on the subjection of men" from whom profits were harvested by those who controlled the laborers, Bellamy for the first time discussed socialism in public:

Why has the name Socialist by which is designated a believer in this renovation of Society, who denies that the world ought to be administered any longer in the interests of darkness and chaos become a byword and a name of reproach?.
. . . .

Is it then, as these claim, absurd to dream of the reign of justice on earth, chimerical to anticipate an era when, by equality in the distribution of the fruits of labor every man at the price of moderate exertion shall be as secure of abundance and comfort of the means of education and recreation as he is today secure in his political rights and independence? . . . There is then enough in the world to support all in abundance if it were equally divided. If the burdens as well as the pleasures of life were apportioned equally among all, then should none labor beyond moderation, and none be utterly idle. This is a social condition which justice demands.
. . . .

If you expect from me . . . a theory of Socialism, if you expect a minute description of that new world of whose peace and liberty and happiness I have told you, you will be disappointed. It is an undiscovered country, no community of men ever assayed its elysian climes, no human footstep has ever trod its shores. The faith of humanity point to its existence. But I know that it exists, and we must find it. . . . [48]

During this same period of intellectual rebelliousness Bellamy also suffered because of the poverty he saw and because of his search for his own religious beliefs. In his notebook of 1871, he describes his search and his Wertherean mood:

For a while, indeed, the young man may remain satisfied with the ideals of truth and duty in which he was bred. Then seeing, or fancying that he sees their insufficiency, he casts them aside and with soul wide open goes through dry places seeking everywhere to find God. He carries his loyalty in his hand anxious only to find some fitting shrine where he may lay it down and be at rest. Then, indeed, as the hopelessness of his search is borne in upon him, come days and nights full of bitterness and blasphemy, of recklessness, and at last of profound life weariness.[49]

From his many journals and from the rough draft of his story about Eliot Carson, one may assemble the many reasons for Bellamy's turmoil and search—and, as one might expect, his loneliness because of his religious family: "I doubt not that often times in New England where people take their religion so earnestly parents of strong dogmatic convictions have suffered more from the irreligious dispositions of children than any satisfactions of parentage can compensate."[50]

The religious discussions of the era centered, as they had in New England since its history began, upon questions of dogma and ritual. One of the best descriptions of such credal diversity and its resulting confusion is presented in Bellamy's fantasy "With the Eyes Shut" (1889). In this story the narrator visits the establishment of Ortor, who specializes in making speaking, time-improving clocks as various as people's ideas about how to improve themselves:

In the religious clock department were to be found Catholic, Presbyterian, Methodist, Episcopal, and Baptist time-pieces, which, in connection with the announcement of the hour and quarter, repeated some tenet of the sect with a proof text. There were also Talmadge clocks, and Spurgeon clocks, which respectively marked the flight of time by phrases taken from the sermons of those eminent divines, and repeated in precisely the voice and accents of the original delivery. In startling proximity to the religious department I was shown the skeptical clocks. So near were they, indeed, that when, as I stood there, the various time-pieces announced the hour of ten, the war of opinions that followed was calculated to unsettle the firmest convictions. The observations of an Ingersoll which stood near me were particularly startling.[51]

Had Bellamy himself been one of the speaking clocks, he, like Herman Melville and Samuel Clemens, would have been unable to reconcile the idea of a benevolent deity with the widespread deviltry and misery that existed in his world. Moreover, Bellamy rebelled at the idea of a god who demanded that man be willing to be damned for His sake and at the belief that the majority of souls went to hell. In the 1870s he wrote that "People who believed in hell-fire doctrine had no right to have children if [they] think that the majority of souls born go to hell. Parents should consider life as distinctly a blessing if they bestow it."[52]

Bellamy also rejected the concept of compensations, since what really mattered was what happened to man while living on the earth. He also scorned the view that development occurred through tribulations and that suffering evoked pity and pity, love. To him, the acceptance of the concept of the benefit of suffering would render charity as opposed to God's will: "The truth is, in the warmth of our human heart, we have nursed a better growth, a more compassionate and loving disposition, a hatred of suffering, that does not accord with, that is, in fine, better than the love of nature and of God."[53] To Bellamy, Christ could not be considered the Savior, nor God responsible for the creation of the world, so long as "this hideous atrocity of life" exists. Christ could be loved, however, if He were "regarded as a man seeking to wipe away tears and to succor those in need."[54] Bellamy finally reasoned in October 1872 that, if the Creator of man gave him instincts, he could at least please Him by "conscientiously fulfilling his instincts one and all, while it is certain that only so can he attain any consistent development whatever." By following this principle, he would find his right place in the universe and be less deceived in his conjectures concerning the "correlation of the parts to the whole." Furthermore, the rudimentary religion he could create would have a hearty hatred of sham and conventionalities and of all attempts at self-conceal- ment and self-misrepresentation. Bellamy, who expressed his firm- ness in his acceptance of this decision, intended no "repetition of the meaningless jingle words about doing right whatever befall"; and he did not intend to pattern his conduct upon the rules of "morality mongers and religionists": he would be "a law unto himself."[55]

By making this decision, Bellamy had resolved the problem of his world, as he had observed it in 1871, that "intellectually speak- ing seems to be living in a sort of hand-to-mouth style"; for, he then observed that,

The Apostle's injunction to 'prove all things, Hold fast that which is good' seems to be consistently obeyed so far as the first is concerned, but no one seems to be in the least able to hold fast anything whatever in the way of abstract truths. . . . I have not the least inclination to doubt the existence of abstract truths because the world has just now discovered the falsity of those it has always held as such and has not yet found any better ones.[56]

Having discovered the falsity of his family's religious beliefs—living in an era that had had such beliefs shaken by Charles Darwin's *The Origin of Species by Means of Natural Selection* (1859) and *The Descent of Man* (1871)—Bellamy, an independent thinker, an introspective man, and a mystic, resolved to solve the mystery of life: "This life is a mystery, men say, and. . . . go about their business. This life is a mystery I say and do no other thing till I solve it in some measure at least. That mystery includes all things, and therefore, until I know what I am doing, I will do nothing. I will not live at random as men do."[57]

The Resolution of the Mystery

The result of Bellamy's resolve to fathom the mysteries of life included man's relationship to God, to his fellowmen, and to the universe. Religion, as he conceived it, "was a man's idea of his relations to the universe around him."[58] He incorporated his philosophy in "Religion of Solidarity" written in 1873, and expressed elements of it in the Eliot Carson notebooks, in some of his novels and short stories, and in sections of his manuscripts and other journals. Rereading the essay in 1887, Bellamy classified it as "crude and redundant in style," but he nonetheless wrote that "this is my ripe judgment of life."[59]

In Bellamy's religion God is no longer to be blindly worshipped on faith by man, the inferior being. The instinct in man to merge himself with others and in nature—to get out of himself, the individual[60]—and to attain the impersonal is the expression of the universal or Infinite in him;[61] and man becomes the manifestation, or the fragment, but not the microcosm, of the All-Soul, or God. Man's body becomes significant because it is the dwelling place of the soul and the channel through which he experiences his universal instincts or intuitions.[62] To Bellamy, "men are the bodies of one god, with one divine essence pervading all in different measures";[63] and, as a result, each man has in him the universal life: "the one soul of all being whereof all are manifestations."

To Bellamy, the ability of men to develop the universal or "not-self" varies, for duality exists in all mankind: one part is his individuality—his personality, his mind, body, appetite—and the other side of him is "something that seems eternal and infinite," which might be called "God, the universe, infinity, or what else seems to imply to our minds the idea of absolute and the all."[65] The universal self becomes evident to the individual through actual experiences and can be cultivated; for, when a man rises above himself, he reaches a state of Infinity—and in this condition of impersonality he obtains an objective view of all individuality and recognizes its smallness.[66] Man develops this impersonality in himself or enters the godhead by meditation and introspection, by deeds of generosity and "self-devotion" (or sacrifice),[67] by realization of the beauties of nature;[68] in these ways he realizes Christ's words "The Kingdom of Heaven is within you," for, when the "mind takes hold on the universe, the soul is conjoined with eternity and God."[69]

Bellamy regarded nature as an "auxiliary to man," and the sensitive person's reaction to it is better proof than Darwin's theory of the "underlying unity and common origin of life."[70] In a manuscript fragment Bellamy described the "physical phenomena . . . as those sentiments of intense and mysterious sympathy excited by sublimity and beauty in nature or in men and in art, whether in repose or in action: The emotions of transport, ecstasy, and trance under the influence of music, of majestic imaginations, of enthusiasms of every class." He then stated that "These mental experiences are distinguished from all others by a certain unearthliness; there is no blood in them; they are marked by what may be called a vague intensity. They are independent of the intellect and unconscious of the being. . . . They seem to rise to a higher vault. . . . over. . . . the animal and mental life. They are, in short, spiritual—different not in degree but in kind from the phenomena of the mind and the body to which no analysis can reduce or assimilate them."[71]

When man achieves the impersonal and rises above himself, he is able to view his individuality objectively; and he then realizes how petty and insignificant are its subjective reactions, which are the result of his self-concern and self-interest. The Infinite not-self makes the life of man more than that of a brute, and it makes his personality, or individuality, "but an eye through which he looks up and becomes conscious of other life, other eyes, other forms and conditions of being than his own."[72] However, Bellamy, the pragmatist, recognized that some people are seemingly incapable of such "soul culture" and also that, if this group did not exist, "we might otherwise have to make slaves of some to get the business done at all"—and with this thought he solved the problem of getting the "dirty work" done that had so concerned him and his cousin William.[73]

Moreover, Bellamy did not believe that individuality should be destroyed, not only because it was dignified by being the "expression of the universal" but also because the centrifugal force preserves "that variety in unity which seems the destined condition of being"[74] and plays its necessary role. To Bellamy, love is developed among human beings by mental or "physical correlation of the individualities"; and sexual relationship is "a proof of the common essence of souls." However, the "lust of soul for soul" that is impossible to fulfill makes such sexual unions imperfect; they are but a "partial realization of soul solidarity."[75] Nonetheless, in one of his notebooks Bellamy indicated that, through love of a woman, a man could begin to realize "What manner of thing the love of a divine being could be. . . ."[76]

Despite Bellamy's experiences with women (mentioned in his journal of 1874 in particular), he feared that marriage forced a man to give "god, nature, and books the go-by" because he had to devote his time to earning a living: "Hitch Pegasus to a family cart and he can't go off the thoroughfare."[77] In *Six to One* (1878) Dr. Brainard tells Edgerton that "Matrimony begins with kisses, but it ends with bread and butter; the mouth is the alpha and omega of the tender passion. It begins by making idealists of us but ends in making us materialists".[78] Because of such materialism, marriage makes men less generous, more grasping, and more unscrupulous.[79]

Bellamy shared these views of marriage quite bluntly with Emma Sanderson, the adopted daughter of the Reverend Bellamy; she was ten years Edward's junior, and he had established a deep friendship with her that developed into "an absurd passion." When Edward told Emma that he would not marry, she began to consort with other young men and eventually became engaged to one of them. Because Bellamy became so moody, so silent, and so coldly polite after Emma's engagement was announced, his mother suggested that Emma stay in Springfield and come to Chicopee Falls only to teach her music students and to sing in the church choir. One Sunday evening as she prepared to join her fiancé to attend the church service, Edward appeared in the room, took Emma in his arms, and said: "You can't go out. You're my little girl, and I can't let anyone else have you."[80] Edward Bellamy and Emma Sanderson were married on 30 May 1882. His marriage constitutes one of the most important events in his life and in his education as a reformer.

A son, Paul Bellamy, was born on 26 December 1884 and a daughter, Marion, on 4 March 1886. Wrote Bellamy in "How I Came to Write 'Looking Backward'," the birth of his children gave the "problem of life a new and more solemn meaning"; he noted that he could not understand parents who did not become "intensely interested in the social question," since they had "to provide for and safeguard their [children's] future when they themselves shall no longer be on earth."[81] As Bellamy has his shadow Eliot Carson say, the birth of his children revealed "his oneness with posterity" and "with manhood": "He cannot thenceforward bear the thought of leaving his children . . . anybody's children, to struggle in such a horrid world as this. Cured once for all of Hermitism and self-absorption, he plunges with enthusiasm, with tremendous earnestness, into the study of social conditions and develops nationalism."[82]

The Journalist

During his stint as a book reviewer and editorial writer for the *Springfield Union* from 1872 to December 1877 Bellamy wrote in his inimitable style many articles and reviews that indicate his knowledge of the thought and problems of his time. No other *Union* contributor compares with him in the use of compound and complex sentences, in the telling analogies from everyday life and nature, in the references made to the "Religion of Solidarity," and in the striking comments often made about books and situations.

In his book reviews Bellamy airs his criticism of style, analyzes the development of character and ideas, and often infuses his own notions of life, literature, and ideology. His reviews include works on women, religion, science, sanitation, housing, biography, history, and much fiction; and his critical comments are often as pithy as those of Edgar Allan Poe, who never spared an author's feelings. Of the novel *Cachet* by M. T. H. Hamilton, Bellamy wrote that "the literary style is beneath criticism";[83] of Anna Thomas's *"He Cometh Not," She Said*, he observed that "the title is the most striking thing about it";[84] and he stated that "Joaquin Miller's work, nominally upon the Modocs, whom he admires, but really and chiefly upon himself whom he admires more, and his wife, whom he admires less, will soon be out."[85] In his editorials which also covered a multiplicity of subjects and often referred to books or magazine articles that he had reviewed, Bellamy demonstrated the clear and logical thinking and the sense of form and style that were to bring him literary success. Both book reviews and editorials suggest Bellamy's indefatigible industry as well as the value of his exposure to such a broad range of knowledge and thought to his career as a novelist and as the creator of an ideal state.

When Bellamy stopped his work for the *Union* in late 1877, he did so for several reasons: he was suffering from fainting attacks; he wished to join his brother Frederick on a trip to the Hawaiian Islands; and he desired to devote himself to a literary career, a decision encouraged by the reception of the fiction he had already published. After Edward and his brother spent three months on their trip to and from Hawaii, Edward devoted the rest of 1878 to writing and publishing seven short stories and three novels. In February 1880 Bellamy, as he later expressed his action to William Dean Howells, forsook "literature . . . and [became] wholly absorbed in money-getting. . . ."[85] He and Charles became proprietors of a newspaper.

The brothers published on 24 February 1880 the first issue of a triweekly, the *Springfield Penny News;* when it became very successful, they changed it in May to the *Daily News*. It was devoted to presenting the news in a style that would save the readers from "reading through a column of words for what might be condensed in one sentence." They declared themselves and their publication free from the pressures that could be exerted by "peremptory stockholders to whose whims and small ambitions" they might have had to bend; and they also made it clear that their paper had "no enemies to vent its spleen upon, . . . no ill humor toward the successful, and no malice for the unfortunate." All in all, they intended to publish "the people's newspaper."[87] They published few articles about the fine arts, literature, or family reunions; but they covered foreign and domestic occurrences, reprinted human-interest stories from publications from California to New York, and sought to present accurate reports about the causes of strikes. During a period of unemployment the editors offered to print free of charge "advertisements for persons desiring situations, or wanting help."[88]

Charles, who was also a lawyer, acted as the publisher of the newspaper; Edward was the editor; but both men "worked heartily in any line that was likely to boom the success of the infant journal."[89] One of Edward's contributions to the *Daily News* was an irregularly published feature, a column recording conversations with a character named Isaac about common problems and concepts. Bellamy had already used the dialogue style in his fiction, and would employ it as well in his utopian novels and in the "Talks on Nationalism" for his reform publication the *New Nation*.

In 1884, because the circulation of the *Daily News* decreased during a depression and because another paper, the *Daily Democrat*, affected its popularity, the brothers considered closing. Edward tried to convince Charles that they should declare insolvency and cease publication; but Charles, with his "pride and combativeness," rejected his brother's suggestions and assumed all financial responsibility for the newspaper's indebtedness to free Edward from any monetary loss.[90] As a result of Charles's generosity and courage, Edward retired from the editorial world to devote himself to "fresh essays in romance."[91]

Non–Utopian and Utopian Novels (1875–1897)

Bellamy had published short stories and novels before and shortly after he ended his career with the *Springfield Union*. His short stories had appeared in such magazines as *Scribner's, Appleton's Journal, Lippincott's, Good Company*, and *Sunday Afternoon*. As a journalist, Bellamy had created a prose style that, as William Dean Howells observed in his introduction to the *Blindman's World and Other Stories* (1898), "did not seek distinction of expression; it never put the simplest and plainest reader to shame by the assumption of those fine gentlemen airs which abash and dishearten more than the mere literary swell can think. . . . But the nobility of the heart is never absent from his work; and he has always the distinction of self-forgetfulness in his art."

The characters in Bellamy's short stories and novels are not highly individualized; they are little more than puppets who are used by their creator to display their psychological or ideological reactions to the situations that have been created to test them. The absence of in-depth portrayals has two causes. First, Bellamy recorded in his Hawaiian notebook that "the impersonal life which all have in common is the only important part of men or women" and that "studying characters as an occupation" would be just as much "bosh" as trying to delineate "the infinitesimal differences between the leaves of a tree." "When you know half a dozen men, you know

all, and when you know three women you know all."[92] Second,
Bellamy's motive for writing was "chiefly to see myself reflected
from the page, to know myself,"[93] as he attempted to "trace the
logical consequences of certain assumed conditions."[94] As he revealed
in "Two Days' Solitary Imprisonment" (1878), his timid and im-
aginative Jacob "had an unprofitable habit of taking every incident
of possible embarrassment or danger that occurred to his mind as
the suggestion for imaginary situations of inconvenience or peril,
which he would then work out [by] fancying how he would feel
and what he would do, with the utmost elaboration, and often with
really more nervous excitement than he would be likely to experience
if the events supposed should occur."[95]

In his first published novel, *Six to One* (1878), Bellamy expressed
his own philosophy about man's relationship to the universal and to
nature—in this case, the sea surrounding Nantucket. When Edgerton, who at thirty is a newspaper's exhausted managing editor,
goes to what he considers a "comatose community" (*SO*, 12), "his
sensitive temperament . . . brought him at once under the influence of the rest and vitality of the sea" (*SO*, 31); for "he seemed
resting on the heaving bosom of infinity and from the contact he
drew a sense of moral, mental, and physical health and balance,
such as he had never known before" (*SO*, 32). As the companion of
six young ladies, Edgerton discovers that women are like "galvanic
batteries" (*SO*, 42); and he writes to his doctor that it seems to him
"that there is a marriage intellectual as well as physical, complex
and social as well as dual and domestic" (*SO*, 43). Like Bellamy in
"Religion of Solidarity," Edgerton thinks that entirely spiritual
unions are as real as those of marriage but that they also create a
higher sense of completion. Of the six young women who entertain
Edgerton, Addie, the youngest and the one who has "strong aesthetic
feelings," associates with and interprets everything in its relationship
to the ocean, for which she has "something like a mystical passion"
(*SO*, 54). When Edgerton takes the girls sailing in his boat *The
Dream*, he notices that Addie is absorbed by the sea with "passionate
sympathy" (*SO*, 57): she has "attained a faculty of sharing to an
unusual degree that calming and elevating communion which all
the grand forms of nature are ready to pour into any human heart
which turns to them in self-forgetfulness for the refreshment that
comes from elevation out of the personal sphere" (*SO*, 81).

Edgerton is also attracted to Kate Mayhew, who hates the island and rejects the sea. She represents imprisonment in individuality. Though he listens to her criticism of the island with sympathy and understanding, he realizes, when he encounters Addie, that what he had felt for Kate had been only pity, not love. Addie, who loves Edgerton and is disturbed because this affection interferes with her devotion to the sea, finally resolves her conflict by surrendering to and accepting Edgerton's love after she is almost drowned in the ocean—and has, of course, been rescued by him. Addie and Edgerton, as the bearers of Bellamy's philosophy, are the most fully— if somewhat generally—delineated characters. Of the other five women, only Kate receives more attention and development.

In *Dr. Heidenhoff's Process* (1878–79), one of the first American psychological novels, Bellamy portrays two characters who have sinned, who are not saved by the church, and who finally commit suicide. Henry Burr, the suitor of Madeline Brand, desires to marry her; but he has agreed to await patiently her recovery from her deep anguish because of her sinful life with her seducer and betrayer Harrison Coris, a Bostonian who had come to town as a drugstore clerk. In a dream Burr visits Dr. Heidenhoff, who has perfected a shock treatment and who succeeds in relieving Madeline of her distress. When Burr awakens, he receives a letter from Madeline in which she not only declares her love for him but also states that, since she is a "soiled rose,"[96] she cannot damage his honor by marrying him. At the end of her letter she tells Henry that "I go this night to that elder and great redeemer, whose name is death" (139). Like George Bayley, the villager who had not been relieved by his anguish because of his theft and who felt that the "blood of Christ" lacked something like "the virtue of Lethe water" (13), Madeline has also committed suicide. Like George, she desired "death, the promise of eternal sleep, rest, and oblivion" (88); for, since repentance while alive had not lessened her distress, she felt that her spirit in heaven would also have suffered because of its memory of her sinfulness (87–88).

Just as unusual for its time as *Dr. Heidenhoff's Process* but in a quite different perspective is Bellamy's historical novel, *The Duke of Stockbridge* (1878–79), which was serialized in the *Berkshire Courier* of Barrington, Massachusetts (and not published as a book until after his death). In this romance Bellamy, who had set the mastery of history as one of his objectives, used a historical incident, Shays'

rebellion (1786–87), not only to indicate his interest in the op-
pressed and their revolt against their exploitation but also to present
an accurate interpretation of the causes of the revolt. In fact, Bellamy's criticisms were applicable to his own period. The farmers of
Massachusetts who had fought in the War of Independence discovered the futility of their battle; for, when they returned home after
their services, they discovered that they had been freed from the
rule of the English kings only to be exploited and tyrannized by
the rich. Their situation was not improved; they were still the
victims of the banker, the storekeeper, and the plutocrats. Despite
the lectures about socialism he had already presented and the pictures
of the socioeconomic inequality and exploitation he had drawn in
The Duke of Stockbridge, Bellamy did not suggest in this novel the
solutions that were to appear in *Looking Backward,* in his articles,
and in *Equality.* The only real value today of this weak romance
with its dialect of the people lies in its having been the first, accurate
portrayal of the causes of Shays' Rebellion.[97]

In *Miss Ludington's Sister* (1884), his last novel before the utopian
Looking Backward, Bellamy created a woman who has lost her youthful beauty because of an unmentioned disease and who has isolated
herself from humanity in a rebuilt home where she idolizes the
miniature ivory portrait made of her before her illness. To Ida
Ludington, the new home on Long Island not only restores her
memories of her youth but also pleases the spirits of her old neighbors
and friends who have died. She has an oil portrait made reproducing
the ivory miniature, and "the frame of the girl's picture she had
wound with deepest crape."[98] A few years after her settlement in
her "ghostly village," Miss Ludington inherits from her deceased
cousin his son, Paul De Riemer, aged two years; and, although she
reluctantly accepts responsibility for him, he wins her heart when
he enters her living room, coos at her portrait, and stretches his
arms toward it. As the boy becomes older and listens to Ida's stories
about the portrait, he becomes so entranced that the beautiful girl
"lighted his first love-dreams" and becomes "his ideal of feminine
loveliness." (21).

When Miss Ludington is more than sixty years old and Paul is
twenty-two and a college graduate, he informs her in a letter that
the girl of the picture is "neither lost nor dead, but a living and
immortal spirit" (25). Paul then explains his belief that every individual passes through many changes and during them develops a

soul, that each of these individual spirits has its own immortality, and that they "one day will meet and be together in God's eternal presence . . . " (31). Miss Ludington is so impressed and overjoyed by Paul's argument about "the immortality of past selves" (36) that she removes the crape from the frame of the oil painting and decorates the picture with "a veritable bower of the white flowers of immortality" (37). When Miss Ludington later meets while shopping an old girlhood friend who had looked so much like her that they had been called "The Twins," she invites the woman, Sarah Cobb Slater, to visit her. When Mrs. Slater visits her, Miss Ludington tells Mrs. Slater about her concept of the immortality of each stage of transformation and of paradise as "not merely a garden of withered flowers! We shall find the rose and lily of our life blooming there" (54).

When Mrs. Slater takes a tour of the house and sees the portrait, she is intrigued by it and wonders how Miss Ludington has acquired it, for she knows the subject of the painting. When Ida and Paul express their ideas about "the immortality of past selves," Mrs. Slater asks why these past selves had never manifested themselves during a "spiritualist séance." Although Paul denounces spiritualism as a fraud and mediums as humbugs, Mrs. Slater eventually convinces him and Ida that the subject of the portrait might appear. Paul and Ida request that she make arrangements for a séance, and she agrees to do so. When Mrs. Slater has a friend send Paul and Ida the address of Mrs. Legrand, the friend tells them that Mrs. Legrand is so impressed with Miss Ludington's desire to "test the question whether our past selves have immortal souls distinct from present selves" (70) that she wishes immediately to arrange a meeting with her and Paul.

During the first séance Mrs. Legrand produces the young Ida of the portrait; the girl recognizes Miss Ludington with tenderness; but she smiles at Paul like a woman, not a spirit. After this session Mrs. Legrand's manager, Dr. Hull, tells Paul and Ida that she is very ill with a serious heart disease that makes her meetings very dangerous for her; and Paul asks what effect her death would have upon the appearing spirit: "would not the already materialized spirit be in a position to succeed to the physical life which the medium relinquished?" As might be expected, the second séance brings about the death of Mrs. Legrand, the spirit of Ida is still materialized, and Paul and Ida invite her to live with them. Paul becomes entranced by her, she treats him with "conventional politeness," and Miss Ludington eventually takes it upon herself to explain to young Ida that the love Paul had for the portrait is now hers.

As a result, young Ida asks Miss Ludington to send Paul to her; when he arrives, they embrace. When Dr. Hull comes to visit with Miss Ludington, he and Paul distress young Ida with their conversation about the duty a man has "to fulfill all reasonable obligations incurred by his past selves" (183) and "to provide . . . [for his future selves] a sound body and good name, if nothing more" (184). When Ida and Paul leave to play croquet, Dr. Hull tells Miss Ludington that, if she dies, young Ida would have no legal recognition because the courts would not "recognize such a relation as exists between you and this young lady" (191). When Miss Ludington asks how young Ida could be recognized as a person by the law, Dr. Hull suggests that the only solution is either adoption or marriage. When Miss Ludington relates the conversation to Paul, he proposes to young Ida, she accepts him, and he no longer worships her as a "semi-spiritual being" but as a woman whom it was not a sacrilege "to kiss a thousand times a day . . ." (204).

Paul's change in his attitude about young Ida is matched by one in her: she is pleased to be loved like an ordinary woman; but she soon begins to cry often, to suffer from moodiness, and then to experience profound dejection. When she does not collaborate in setting the date of their wedding, Paul decides that the basic problem is the "conflict between the love of the woman which went out to her earthly lover, and would fain make him happy, and the nature of the inhabitant of heaven, where there is neither marrying or giving in marriage" (223). When Paul explains this view to young Ida, she listens with astonishment, then with an "overpowering sense of shame," and abruptly leaves him. Thereafter she reveals in letters the chicanery of Dr. Hull, who is actually her father, Mr. Slater, and she confesses that she had learned about Miss Ludington from her mother, Mrs. Slater. She also declares her love for Paul and her gratitude for Miss Ludington's affection and kindness, as well as her own "deadly sickness at . . . heart" (236): she admits that, though she had arrived in their home as a "frivolous girl," she was leaving it "a broken-hearted woman" (243).

After Paul and Miss Ludington have advertised and searched for Ida, she is finally located; she is convinced that they have forgiven her; she and Paul are eventually married; and Miss Ludington dies in her sleep with "features relaxed in a smile of joyous recognition" (258)—a smile that indicates that she has been met in the heavenly world by her former selves. When she had talked to young Ida about death, she had said more than once that "It is very strange to see people who dread death always looking foward for it instead of backward. In their fear of dying once they quite forget that they have died already many times. It is the most foolish of all things to imagine that by prolonging the career of the individual, death is kept at bay. The present self must die in any case by the inevitable process of time, whether the body be kept in repair for later selves or not. The death of the body is but the end of the daily dying that makes up earthly life" (256).[99]

Journalist Become Prophet

As was Bellamy's technique in many of the short stories and in *Dr. Heidenhoff's Process,* in which strange worlds are visited in dreams, the visit to the world of the year 2000 that is made in *Looking Backward* (1888) by the central character and narrator Julian West under hypnotic trance identifies the changes that have taken place after the passage of more than a century. This future, written during a period of serious depression and unemployment in the United States, so intrigued Bellamy's readers that *Looking Backward* not only became a best-seller in the United States but was also translated into almost every language of the world—a story that is related in *Edward Bellamy Abroad: An American Prophet's Influence* (1962).

The picture of a new world that resolved many of the social, economic, and moral problems of Bellamy's own era so impressed its viewers, in fact, that they desired to make it reality. The last chapter of this study will be concerned with the influence of the book upon society and upon specific individuals. But its effect upon Bellamy's life and preoccupations must also be identified. Its success led him to devote himself not only to utopian works but to nonfiction publications and, reticent and retiring though he had always been, to public speaking. The employees of the *Union* who had known him during his years with the newspaper noted that the success of *Looking Backward* had made him more genial, earnest, and sympathetic when he conversed with others: he had lost his coat of thistles.

In June 1888 Cyrus Willard, a journalist and a Theosophist, wrote to Bellamy that he desired to found a club for the discussion and propagation of the ideas presented in *Looking Backward;* and, when Bellamy responded on 4 July, he informed Willard that he had had a comparable proposal from Sylvester Baxter, a well-known editorial writer. He suggested that Willard and Baxter, who were associated with the *Boston Globe* and the *Boston Herald,* respectively, work together to form such an organization. To Bellamy, the formulation of the club in Boston seemed particularly appropriate: as the scene of the Tea Party and the center of abolitionism it was the proper place also for the beginning of the third movement for the liberation of people.

On 8 January 1889 the first meeting of the Boston Bellamy Club was held at Tremont House. The fifty members present not only elected officers but also adopted principles which became the unifying statement of Bellamy clubs organized nationwide. In February 1889 the publication committee of the Boston Bellamy Club successfully recommended that the Nationalist Education Association be formed with Bellamy as president, that it publish a monthly magazine, the *Nationalist,* and that this publication provide not only educational material but also the national news of the movement. When the Boston Bellamy Club celebrated its first anniversary in December 1889 at Tremont Temple, Bellamy spoke about the principles and purposes of Nationalism; and, at the second anniversary meeting, two thousand people heard him speak about the methods of Nationalism.

The founders of the Bellamy Club had selected members very slowly in order to include only individuals who had time to work with them, money to support the organization, or the influence to spread its ideas. Cyrus Willard and Laurence Gronlund asserted that the membership was drawn from the cultivated and the well-to-do, and Henry Ford noted that the members of such clubs were not "the debtor and the malcontent." Because many writers, publishers, and editors from all sections of the United States supported Nationalism, much attention was given the organizations; and, as a result, an article of 1890 in the *North American Review* stated that, after tariff and the speakership, the subjects of greatest interest to Americans were Nationalism and electric lighting. Because of the popularity of Nationalism, many of the leaders of the clubs began to think that the educational endeavors of the organizations were no longer needed and that the time had arrived for political action to begin.

In April 1891 the *Nationalist* had to cease publication because of financial problems. The failure provided Bellamy, who had not had much respect for the publication, the opportunity to found his own weekly paper, one that would be devoted to the "discussion of the industrial and social situation from the moral and economic view indicated" by *Looking Backward*. Because Bellamy secured the subscription list of the *Nationalist* and collected many other names from his correspondence, the *New Nation,* which first appeared in January 1891, reached eight thousand subscribers. One of its most significant columns was "Talks on Nationalism" which Bellamy wrote under the pen name of Mr. Smith; these articles not only provided material later used in *Equality* but advocated the objectives of the People's Party (discussed in chapter 5). However, Bellamy did not believe that the Nationalist clubs should become wholly political, for he deemed that only *steps* toward the achievement of an ideal state could be achieved by any political party.

Bellamy ceased the publication of the *New Nation* in February 1894. He had profited greatly as editor of the paper because he had not only become aware of the criticism of the ideas of *Looking Backward* but had also answered his critics. As a result of this intellectual experience he was better prepared for his last utopian novel, *Equality* (1897), in which he not only answered his critics but also supplied the information omitted from *Looking Backward* relative to the way the ideal state was to be achieved. *Equality* is clear and informative, but also somewhat boring. As a result, this last important book about the year 2000 has unfortunately been ignored by many Bellamy readers who, if they had read it, would have had greater understanding of what he desired to achieve in the ideal state.

While Bellamy was writing this second utopian novel, he was suffering from tuberculosis. He died 22 May 1898. A physically afflicted man during most of his life, Bellamy had intellectual strength and left to the world two crucial utopian novels, novels that both influenced the general socioeconomic development of the United States and halted the growth of Marxism during one of the country's most critical periods, the 1930s.

Chapter Two
The Basic Aims and Principles of the Ideal Society

In 1935, Edward Weeks, editor of the *Atlantic Monthly,* asked Charles Beard, the famous historian, and John Dewey, the philosopher and educator, to join him in preparing lists of the "twenty-five most influential books published since 1885." All three men placed *Looking Backward* second only to Marx's *Das Kapital.*[1] In the same period Louis Boudin, social scientist and Marxist, asserted in his address during a Communist convention that *Looking Backward* and the Nationalists were "an influential factor in retarding the growth of our movement during its entire existence of some forty-odd years. The history of the Utopianism of our movement has never been told. When it is told, it will form an interesting story, and to many a surprising one. For this ideology influenced people whom no one would ordinarily suspect being subject to its influence."[2]

Although the Marxists condemned Bellamy as being "unscientific," Bellamy's evolutionary program had more appeal to Americans because its specific aims and its basic democratic principles were those of the Declaration of Independence, because it respected the moral and ethical principles of Christianity, and because it promoted the welfare of all citizens—not just the proletariat. His rational presentation of the Counter Revolution insisted first upon the intellectual and spiritual development of the citizenry, and avoided a world ridden with hatred, persecution, chicanery, and pure materialism by developing a cooperative society based upon the desires of the citizens and their humanitarianism. Even more important, Bellamy, unlike Marx, did not depict the "class of government" that would result from his Counter Revolution; instead, he indicated that the former American government had been further developed and could develop still more when the citizenry so desired.

As has been more thoroughly indicated in *Edward Bellamy Abroad* and in *The Year 2000,*[3] Bellamy, the editorial and book-review writer of the *Springfield Union,* as well as the avid reader, was well acquainted with the works of Marx and with others who also sponsored collective ownership. Although Marx's *Das Kapital* had not yet been published in English when Bellamy wrote *Looking Backward,* he had published reviews of the works about Marx by Harriet Martineau and Stephen Pearl Andrews. Moreover, Bellamy's own intellectual development relative to socialism and solidarity, his concern about the societal environment of his children, and his ethical and moral religious concepts caused him to develop as his own the aims and the principles that belonged to the ideological social fund that had been contributed to by utopists, philosophers, and political economists before and during his own day.

To mention but a few of the sources for his ideas Bellamy, reviewing Professor Crocker's *The Theistic Conception of the World,* wrote that the author believed that man's crowning achievement would be "the establishment of human government on the basis of liberty, equality, and human brotherhood."[4] And his review not only of Charles Nordhoff's *The Communistic Societies of the United States* (1875) but of works by Robert Owen and Etienne Cabet informed him about economic equality and collective ownership.[5] Bellamy both reviewed Edward Bulwer-Lytton's *The Coming Race* and often mentioned it in his reviews; he also wrote an editorial in the *Union* entitled "The Church of the Future According to Matthew Arnold." In this editorial (8 June 1877) Bellamy wrote that Arnold's *Last Essays on Church and Religion* contained the idea that the church be transformed into a national society for the diffusion of goodness and that the Kingdom of God reign among men of the higher type of life. On 7 November 1877 Bellamy reviewed the Reverend Thomas Starr King's *Christianity and Humanity,* which, he said, "kindles musty hearts with the enthusiasm of humanity" and spiritualizes "sordid souls with a sense of God."

The Aims of the New Society

William Graham Sumner thought that the evolution of society would take care of itself. Bellamy disagreed with him and also with reformers who, like the characters of Hawthorne's *Blithedale Romance,* believed that their particular reform would resolve all problems. To correct the ills of the commercial and industrial world, Bellamy believed that his solution had to be so complete that it would include and cover all aspects of the problems;[6] if it did not, his plan would not accord with the ideas of Comte and would be a failure—a failure because of its incomplete coverage. Since the deplorable economic condition was a natural outgrowth of the capitalistic, industrial system which was itself an evolutionary system, one tending toward consolidation, Bellamy's scientific answer was to direct the evolution of the system into channels that would make the results beneficial rather than destructive to mankind.

Because of their importance to the citizenry of a democratic society Bellamy incorporated the principles of the Declaration of Independence, as well as those of Locke and Jefferson that gave the people the right to rebel against an inadequate government and to change it. Bellamy also wished to include the Jeffersonian concept that religion, morality, and education were necessary not only for good government but for the happiness of mankind. Moreover, the spiritual and social goal to be achieved was supplied by Bellamy's "Religion of Solidarity," for his ideal state had to have as an ideological basis the development of the universal in man, his selflessness, his enthusiasm for and his self-sacrifice for humanity and for the social order that depended upon his cooperation.

In seeking to create the ideal society that would fulfill these aims, Bellamy tested ideas pragmatically, for he believed that "No truth can avail unless practically applied."[7] His knowledge of the economic, social, and political life of the nation in his own era led him to recognize how the actualities contrasted with the principles upon which the American government had been founded. As he searched for new and practical instruments that would protect the democratic principles and yet free mankind from the materialism and the thralldom that the industrial world of the machine had created, he found part of his answer in the very system he sought to improve: he saw "a stream of tendencies through ever larger experiments in concentration and combination toward the ultimate complete integration of the nation for economic as well as for political purposes."[8] Since the economic reasons for consolidation were valid and workable, Bellamy accepted this tendency of the times as a "basic principle of association";[9] and he later defended Nationalism's plan as having nothing in it that did not "already exist as a germ or a vigorous shoot in the present order."[10] Bellamy conceived his Counter Revolution as being sponsored by an evolutionist who wished not only to combat the subversive forces that corrupted government for monetary gain but also to change that government for the service and protection of mankind.

Political Institutions

Just as Bellamy had questioned the religious beliefs he had been taught by his Baptist family, so did he review the political institutions that the American forefathers had formulated as a practical and workable means of protecting the ideals expressed in the Declaration of Independence. He felt they had now to be changed to fit not an agrarian but an industrial world—its present environment—and be a positive force for the good of all, not a negative one that suppressed rather than stimulated its citizenry.

In his analysis of the government that had worked well when its citizens had been predominantly agrarian, Bellamy asserted that the government had been distorted by corrupt commercial interests which had used it and robbed it for their own gain and had thereby caused it to fail as the preserver and the guardian of the rights, liberties, and properties of the other citizens. But commercial interests were not alone: in his editorials he had argued that the indifference of the public, as well as its prevalent immoralities and false values, were also responsible for such corruption. To solve the problem, not only the power of wealth had to be harnessed or destroyed but the people had to be aroused to take a "vivid interest" in the administration of the government by giving to it "Interests that vitally concern the everyday life of the people."[11] The solution was, therefore, to combine the citizen's "practical interests with his politics" so that he would give the same attention to the political system that he had always bestowed on his own personal interests and welfare.[12]

The government had to evolve in such a manner that it could be used to reconstruct society, to prevent corruption, and to restore all the liberties and equalities that had been destroyed by the trusts and the syndicates.[13] In such a government the Bill of Rights and the Declaration of Independence would not only have new meaning in the life of every citizen but men would be free and equal for the first time in the history of the world. Because the citizens would enjoy and wish to maintain such educational and cultural opportunities, such economic security, and such reestablished liberties and moralities, they would be alert safeguards of the democracy and would prevent demagoguery. Moreover, because of these same acquired characteristics and opportunities, these truly freed individuals would live in harmony and develop their minds and souls.

Although Bellamy applied Darwin's theory of evolution and although he wished to provide for the survival of what he called, echoing Thomas Huxley, "the truly fittest," he also depended upon the will of politically and economically enlightened humanitarians to bring about such a new order. In his trust in the triumph of the reason of enlightened man as a means of securing social and economic security, Bellamy was akin to such men of his own era as John Fiske—who became so optimistic because of the theory of evolution that he anticipated the perfection of the human soul—and Lester Ward—who also believed that the will and the reason of man should control social and governmental evolution.

The Great Capitalist

Although the government that Bellamy envisioned for his ideal society had as its prerequisite and its foundation the democratic government of the United States, there was to evolve from it a federal democratic socialist government which would replace the capitalists and the monopolies by being the Great Capitalist or the Great Monopoly, for all means of production and distribution would be supported and controlled by the government. This new system would be both an industrial and an economic democracy, for the combination would produce "a systematized, centralized, interlocking organization of the highest efficiency" (LB, 41–42; E, 203).[14] Since the ultimate control of the political and economic life of the nation would be " 'of the people, by the people, and for the people,' and for all of them equally," the citizens would become both the masters and the servants[15] of the nation—for they would assume

the conduct of their own business just as one hundred odd years before they had assumed the conduct of their own government. . . . At last, strangely late in the world's history, the obvious fact was perceived that no business is so essentially the public business as the industry and commerce on which the people's livelihood depends, and that to entrust it to private persons to be managed for private profit is a folly similar in kind, though vastly greater in magnitude, to that of surrendering the functions of political government to kings and nobles to be conducted for their personal glorification. (LB, 41–42)

The Great Monopoly was based upon the application of the democratic principle of self-government, "self-help, self-control, and self-regulation"[16] by the people of their common heritage for the joint interests and welfare of the citizens and of the wealth of the country which was held indivisibly in common (*LB,* 163; *E,* 27). To Bellamy, men had no individual right to a title of any section of the earth, to its product, to its resources and its riches, or to the results of the power of the social organism except as shared ones. He regarded all men, weak or strong, as just as much the equal heirs of their social and economic heritage as they were beneficiaries of equal protection in time of war.[17] This common heritage included not only all the land but also all the inventions and all the machinery that made production possible. (*E,* 87–91).

The Rights of Individuals

When the Great Capitalist had reclaimed the "heritage of the people" that had been plundered and controlled by the monopolies that had also threatened to manage the government, specific changes had to be inaugurated that would specify what the citizens of the ideal state might personally own and consider to be their private property. Every citizen, as a partner in the nationalized industries, had his stock in the government; and his stock became his at birth and lasted until his death (*E,* 117). From this stock he drew a dividend, which became his annual income; and he had an inalienable right to spend it in any fashion except for private profit. Aside from this possession, he also owned the household and personal effects that he had acquired by spending his annual income (*LB,* 92; *E,* 117–21). Since the citizens could spend their stipends as they desired, Bellamy argued, as did Ferdinand Lassalle and Lawrence Gronlund,[18] that ownership had not been destroyed but had been made a certainty; and it was not the sham it frequently had been in the nineteenth century. During that era the "sacred-right of property" (*E,* 121) had been a hollow phrase in comparison with its significance in the new government to which the "modern ethics of wealth . . . deduce the rights of property from the rights of man" (*E,* 113). In Bellamy's 2000 it was thought that, if men had a right to live, they also had a right to the income from the natural resources, the inventions, and the products of the nation for their sustenance.

Bellamy defended his definition of private property after its presentation in *Looking Backward* in speeches, in articles, and more extensively in *Equality*. In these works he affirmed that, instead of abolishing private property, the new government had really established it for the first time and that only private capitalism had been abolished (*E*, 117).[19] One of his most effective explanations was an analogy in which he showed that nineteenth-century individuals who owned stock in large corporations had permitted their property to be managed for them and had drawn large dividends; and this system was necessitated by the state's ownership of all productive and distributive facilities (*E*, 118). Bellamy also argued that legal title to property in the nineteenth century had not entailed a moral right when it had not been earned but inherited or when it had been procured in an evil or an antisocial way.[20] To the argument that every one had a right to what he or she produced, Bellamy's reply was that in cooperative labor—whether for a private or a government concern—it was impossible to determine with accuracy exactly what amount of the production was due to one person's efforts and ingenuity and how much had actually been contributed by others (*E*, 107). But, added Bellamy, no matter how unequal the abilities of a person might be, this difference could never entail the moral right for men to use their ability, or the power it earned them, to enslave others (*E*, 107, 108).

Although all the homes of the year 2000 were owned by the government and the citizens had to rent them, they received a title to them that was even more significant than the ones given them during the nineteenth century despite the fact that they had no right to sublet their residences.[21] Bellamy cagily argued that in prior times a home had not really been owned when it was mortgaged and that, when the mortgage had been paid, the owner possessed his house only as long as he paid taxes upon it to the government (*E*, 118). To Bellamy, the title to property in the ideal state was psychologically beneficial; it gave men security, freed them from worry, and destroyed jealousy and other antisocial reactions that were so divisive because of the economic inequalities that had once existed (*E*, 120, 27).

To maintain equality of ownership, inheritance of anything but personal effects—which could not be sold and which, from the standpoint of storage space, might be more of a curse than a blessing to the heirs—was discontinued (*LB*, 92–93). In this fashion the backbone and the basis of the property system, which had frequently been based not upon the efforts of the possessor but upon those of relatives, were undermined (*E,* 109). Bellamy's attitude toward inheritance was not new, for in 1873 he had recorded in the *Union* that "modern warfare" upon the right of inheritance struck at the very foundation of accumulated wealth,[22] and he had written in his notes on Blackstone that the right of inheritance was not a natural one.[23] Despite these views, Bellamy, the realist about human nature, had also noted in a journal that the banishment of inheritance would not destroy the urge of men to accumulate the power of wealth;[24] and, as will be seen, he established other satisfactions to replace this human desire.

Responsibilities of the Great Monopoly

Like Jefferson and the other fathers of the American Constitution, Bellamy believed that the government should be concerned with the common good of all citizens and that the best government was not only that which (to paraphrase Jonathan Swift) made the most grass to grow but that which furthered the happiness and the morality of its citizens. The duty of the government to its citizens was an essential part of Bellamy's plan. He developed the theme of its duty and purpose in *Looking Backward* and expanded his ideas about the government's evolution in order to defend these responsibilities in articles and in *Equality.* Although Bellamy was concerned about the political and economic aspects of his ideal government, he was more deeply interested in the effects his socioeconomic plan would have upon the personal lives of the citizens (as will be seen in chapter 4).

The institution of the Great Capitalist had as its aim and its responsibility the establishment of a society in which the intellectual, social, and financial welfare of the citizens would be achieved and in which class and economic conflicts would no longer exist since they had resulted from private capitalism (*E,* 117). To Bellamy, Christianity, civilization, and government existed for the purpose of suppressing the inborn qualities of mankind which made individuals desire to oppress their fellowmen; and he agreed with Thomas Huxley that the highest state of civilization to be attained was one in which the struggle to live was least existent. For Bellamy and his brother Charles,[25] the organic evolution of the American government which was to be promoted by its citizens would lead to the realization that a nation was a union of people for the purpose of using their collective power for their common welfare in all ways.[26]

During the nineteenth century, the government had been primarily concerned with guarding its citizens from external foes and from their criminal fellowmen; and this role had required large military and police forces, innumerable laws, and complicated judicial machinery (*LB*, 44–45; *E*, 9–10, 74). To correct and improve the role of the government, which had given little attention to the brutal struggle for existence in which most of its citizens were involved, Bellamy proposed that its major responsibility in the year 2000 was to be involved with internal affairs and with providing "the highest degree of happiness and welfare for its citizens" by using its collective power against hunger, cold, thirst, and sickness.[27] By accepting this role, the government was safeguarding the highest rights of every citizen: the right to life and to self-preservation (*E*, 73–75). By guaranteeing the economic basis of life by giving equal protection to all its citizens, the government of the year 2000 became not only a universal employment bureau but a great insurance company (*E*, 77–78).[28]

As Bellamy made very, very clear in *Equality*, the will of the majority of individuals was to be safeguarded and expressed:

The popular will is expressed in two ways, which are quite distinct and relate to different provinces: First, collectively, by majority, in regard to blended, mutually involved interests, such as the large economic and political concerns of the community; second, personally, by each individual for himself or herself in the furtherance of private and self-regarding matters. The Government is not more absolutely servant of the collective will in regard to the blended interests of the community than it is of the individual convenience in personal matters. It is at once the august representative of all in general concerns, and everybody's agent, errand boy, and factotum for all private ends. Nothing is too high or too low, too great or too little, for it to do for us. (*E*, 57–58)

The Basic Foundations of the Year 2000

In *Looking Backward* Bellamy compared the government of the nineteenth century to a pyramid which, resting on its apex, was held in this unnatural position by props and guy ropes that were thousands of laws. In the year 2000 the government was resting instead on its natural base because of two innovations: economic equality and the industrial army. As the cornerstone of the new government, economic equality became the foundation of all the freedoms and equalities of the democratic government and the means by which the government fulfilled its duty to its citizens by securing their right to life and security (*LB,* 17, 70, 72; *E,* 27–28, 73–79, 273, 332–33).[29] As for the citizens who worked, whom Bellamy unfortunately termed "the industrial army," they were the organization that produced the means of production and distribution that were the bases of economic equality and that also pledged its fulfillment. As will be noted, Bellamy defended these two innovations by showing that they and the new government that resulted had democratic, ethical, and economic bases and that economic equality was the evolutionary result and the fulfillment of the republic that had been created by the Declaration of Independence of 1776.[30]

Like his predecessor and contemporary Walt Whitman, Bellamy regarded all history as the struggle of man for freedom; and, as a reader who had always been interested in history, he sketched in his works what men had accomplished in this struggle that eventually created the American Revolution and the Declaration of Independence.[31] Bellamy divided the history of the American democracy into two periods: the negative phase, during which it was merely a political substitute for monarchy and was really a pseudorepublic that degenerated into a plutocracy; and the positive phase during which the republican form of government evolved into democratic state socialism (*E,* 14, 18–19).[32] The history of the struggle for freedom in the United States consisted of three periods: (1) the American Revolution, which won political freedom from the British and political equality for the people; (2) the Civil War, which emancipated the black chattel slave; (3) and the Nationalist period, which was to emancipate all citizens from economic and industrial slavery by instituting true social, economic, and political democracy.[33]

The negative phase of the democracy had been caused by two factors: the American forefathers who had drafted the Constitution had not carried their idea of the "inalienable equality" of men to its logical conclusion, economic equality; and they had failed to do so, in part, because they could not foresee the industrial revolution and the effect its economic inequality would have in distorting and destroying the freedom and the rights of men.[34] As a result of this lack of penetration or clairvoyance, the United States had become a house divided; for the spirit of republican equality had dwelt with that of mastership. As a result, the mastery of the rich had created, with a revolution of its own, an industrial and commercial plutocracy that had destroyed the republic.[35] In this oligarchy the minority, the rich, had ruled the majority—the workers and the professional people—and social equality had degenerated into caste and class, master and servant, rich and poor.[36]

Because of the unequal distribution of wealth and power, the political equality and the power of the voters had been destroyed— as had been equality before the law, education, personal liberty, dignity, and freedom. Moreover, because of the control by the plutocrats of the churches, the newspapers, the schools, and the businesses of the country, the freedom of progressive religious and political teaching had been curtailed, as well as freedom of speech and enterprise. To correct the existing situation and to begin a truly positive period of democracy, Bellamy proposed both negative and positive aims and actions. Negatively, the Counter Revolution would end forever the political, commercial, financial, and industrial domination and exploitation of mankind for profit; positively, it would establish the "Four Freedoms": (1) freedom of speech and expression; (2) freedom to worship as one pleased; (3) freedom from fear; (4) freedom from want that would provide everyone a healthy, peaceful life (*E,* 20, 22–23, 73–79, 316, 406–7).

To Bellamy, the true spirit and principles were expressed in the quotation from the Declaration of Independence which "logically contained the entire statement of the doctrine of universal economic equality guaranteed by the nation collectively to its members individually":

We hold these truths to be self-evident; that all men are created equal with certain inalienable rights; that among these are life, liberty, and the pursuit of happiness; that to secure these rights governments are instituted among men, deriving their just powers from the consent of the governed; that whenever any form of government becomes destructive of these rights it is the right of the people to alter or to abolish it and institute a new government, laying its foundations on such principles and organizing its powers in such form as may seem most likely to effect their safety and happiness.[37]

In summary, Bellamy thought that political equality had to be joined with economic equality; for, without "this corollary and necessary supplement," the United States government would "forever fail to secure to a people the equalities and liberties which it promises" (*E*, 18).[38]

Economic Equality: Method and Ascertainment

By economic equality, Bellamy meant that each member of the nation who worked, or who was mentally or physically incapable of working or who was too immature to do so, would draw as his stock in the nationally owned enterprises an annual income that would be equal to that of every mature citizen. Although this income began with birth, the bodily reqirements of children were less than those of adults; and they received, therefore, a smaller initial income.[39] An adult citizen who wished to retire from national service for personal reasons such as study could do so if he would agree to live upon a fourth or a half of his annual income, (*LB*, 213–14); and those who wished to devote themselves to publishing books or newspapers had to save, with the knowledge of the government, funds from their annual stipend to do so.[40] And, although the government encouraged its adults to exert the greatest variety of tastes in the expenditure of income, the person who desired a larger or more luxurious home had to pay for it and limit other expenditures (*LB*, 69). The adults who were incapable of living within their annual income and who overspent it before the year ended were given either a guardian or a friend who could supervise their expenditures (*LB*, 213–14; *E*, 31).

The method used to determine the annual sum allotted to the citizens was to divide the estimated cost of the provisions and services that were expected to be necessary for the nation by the total population. The annual account of each citizen was a credit in the national bank, the only one that remained in operation, which kept the records of expenditures and which balanced and closed each account at the end of every year. In order to expend the money credited to an account, the citizen used, in *Looking Backward*, his credit card and, in *Equality*, spent the desired amounts by writing vouchers,[41] a system comparable to checking accounts. Although the term "dollar" was retained in the new state as a convenient symbol of value, the credit-card system destroyed not only the usage and value of money but also the former credit system; for each person debited his own income account.

When the credit, interest, and profit systems were destroyed because they were socially and economically evil, banks and banking were no longer the heart of the business world. With the banishment of the banks, masses of workers were returned to productive work; the business crises that had afflicted the nation because of extended credit and bank failures no longer occurred; and the ruthless speculation that had exploited the hardworking savers was ended (*LB*, 58, 72, 82, 105, 107; *E*, 24, 33). To Bellamy, faith had been a necessary corollary to the former credit system; for, as soon as doubt appeared, panic ensued, a rush on the banks occurred, and the result was destruction and destitution to businesses and individuals because of financial loss and the paralysis of production (*LB*, 262–63).[42] During such a period money became scarce, and the rates of interest rose to such heights that the harrowed, haggard faces of the citizens reflected their lost homes because of unemployment and the rapacious greed of the moneylenders.[43] Such greed, such unemployment, and such panics were to be avoided in the new state; for, since production and distribution had achieved stability, the only thing that could diminish the supply would stem from such natural causes as drought or seasonal storms. The government would prepare, however, for such disasters by maintaining a surplus of staple foods.

When Bellamy was criticized for his policy of economic equality by Socialists, economists, and radicals as being impractical, he answered that he had rejected the Socialist and the Communist plans of sharing the wealth of the nation according to the individual's need and deed because he believed in "from all equally, to all equally"; and he sustained this belief because no other method of distribution would be morally, economically, and politically satisfactory in a democratic nation.[44] In his articles and speeches Bellamy defended economic equality upon these three principles; and he incorporated these arguments in *Equality*. Because he sought parallels in the life of the nineteenth century to validate the practicality of his plan, his views are of value because they indicate the possible sources of his ideas.

Politically, Bellamy regarded economic equality as the only method of solving the problems of the just wage, of the corruption of government by wealth, of the social instability and immorality, and of the economic wastes of the era. He believed that the "simple formula is the only practicable way of dealing with a large problem,"[45] and he maintained that this solution was consonant, as has been noted, with the aims of the democratic government. Since the government existed to secure the life and welfare of the citizens and since they had the power and the right to change the government that was to serve them, they also had to be considered justified in sharing equally the results of their labor.[46]

Bellamy thought that economic equality would be the means of establishing the stability and the wise ordering of the government; for he had observed that, when people became wholly dependent for their economic welfare upon the government, they would have an impassioned interest in it and would thenceforth be alert, active citizens.[47] Moreover, both political and social solidarity were achieved by economic equality since no man could hurt another without hurting himself and his own welfare, and this situation made it obligatory for each citizen to consider the welfare of the whole— the primal principle of democracy and of the Golden Rule (*E,* 25, 27, 28).[48] In an excellent passage in *Equality* describing economic equality as the cornerstone of the new state (*E,* 17), Bellamy ended with this question: "What form of happiness, so far as it depends at all on material facts, is not bound up with economic conditions; and how shall an equal opportunity for the pursuit of happiness be guaranteed to all save by a guarantee of economic equality?"

To the proud and sensitive Bellamy, happiness and liberty meant "the right not only to live, but to live in [financial] independence of one's fellows" and family (*E,* 27). Such financial independence was impossible in the nineteenth century: children and women were dependent upon others since they were employed at wages below the subsistence level, and men had to bargain against one another for work in the labor market that was controlled by the "Masters of the Bread." In this situation human dignity and decency were lost; people became not only slaves to others but to their own physical needs; and they could not voice their opinions without fear (*E,* 79). Morally, mankind no longer had to beg, steal, and cheat in order to survive; thus the intellectual and spiritual development of humanity was made possible. However, each individual was ethically bound to contribute his labors to the state from which he and his fellow citizens received their livelihood; and, because of the equality of opportunities of all kinds, jealously and other maladjustments were banished. As a result, the individual could enjoy many free-doms that had not existed in the old order.

Freedom of Expression

Because of their economic and political security, the citizens of the year 2000 could enjoy freedom of speech; but they had to make specific arrangements with the government if they desired to publish newspapers or books. If, for example, they desired to spend some of their annual income to publish a newspaper or a journal, they could arrange with the government to save so much of their income each year to defray the expenses of getting subscriptions for their publication and to reimburse the state for the lost service of the editor hired to work for them. Bellamy insisted that, although such a publication was printed by the government-owned organization, no censorship could be exerted by either private or government groups (E, 79–82, 107–8, 99–101; LB, 149, 216, 272).[49] When a citizen wished to criticize the government or public affairs of any kind, he could, at his own expense, publish either a pamphlet or a book—the means of airing his views that Bellamy deemed to be more appropriate than a newspaper. In *Looking Backward* Bellamy had criticized the newspapers of his day for their flippancy, preju-dices, crudeness, and bitterness about government policies and sta-tistics (LB, 133–34); for, as he had indicated in his editorials of the 1870s, he had harbored not only comparable opinions of such publications but had also supported freedom of the press. To Bel-lamy, Professor Sumner of Yale had correctly assessed the policy of the newspapers of his day when he had stated that their aim seemed to be "to throw mud on a man, anyway, and if it doesn't belong to him, he can scrape it off" (LB, 133–34).

Bellamy thought that the morbid, cynical, and negative attitudes expressed in the criticisms of his era enervated instead of stimulating the minds of the readers by presenting constructive, practical, and positive suggestions.[50] To Bellamy, the duty of every citizen was to study the affairs of the nation so that he could "intelligently choose that course which to him" seemed best "calculated to advance the national welfare."[51] In order to judge the merits of political issues, Bellamy agreed with Professor Sumner that political science should be taught in educational institutions; for, to Bellamy, "A modern free government is a government by criticism."[52] Moreover, if the views of the citizens were suppressed and denied expression, the people would eventually express themselves with the "inarticulate roar of the mob" and in "a riotous manner."[53]

As a result, Bellamy also made provisions for the citizens to hold meetings, debates, and discussions in halls that they rented from the government; and in *Equality* (as will be noted in the next chapter) Bellamy added additional precautions as a means of protecting not only the public's expression of opinion but its assertion of its will.

Chapter Three

The Achievement, Form, and Functions of the Ideal State

Although Bellamy portrayed his ideal state in *Looking Backward,* he delayed until *Equality* his presentation of the Counter Revolution and some details about the form and functions of the government. But he also made it very clear that what he presented might not necessarily be what the people desired to create, for time would influence possible developments suited to their needs. When reporters asked Bellamy why he had not portrayed in *Looking Backward* the way the ideal state was to be created, he replied that, when a man wanted to marry, one showed him the beautiful woman but did not tell him about all the problems that marriage entailed. This analogy was illustrative of Bellamy's method, for he believed that individuals had to have a clear idea of what they desired before they planned how to attain it. As he wrote in his notebook, "the discussion of means logically follows not precedes the discussion of ends."[1]

In *Looking Backward,* Bellamy had proposed that the new state had evolved from the tendency toward consolidation which had resulted in the "universal partnership of the people." Having been taught that such an evolution was the sole means of their salvation, the people had, because of their enthusiasm for humanity (their religious awakening), conducted a peaceful uprising that had peacefully instituted the ideal society.[2] Needless to say, Bellamy's critics were not pleased with just a picture of "a moral and material transformation." Those who viewed it favorably desired a blueprint of the way to achieve the new order; but those who disliked it declared that Bellamy had not described the steps to achieve the ideal state, which was, after all, "a mere place in the clouds."[3]

As a result of the popularity and influence of *Looking Backward,* as well as the attitudes of his critics, Bellamy realized that he could not too long "put the people off with generalities when they begin to ask what to do."[4] He soon began to offer specific measures in articles in the *Nationalist,* in speeches, and in the *New Nation.* The next step was to write *Equality,* which was to depict "why and how the Revolution came, the moral and economic causes which compelled and justified it, and finally the steps by which the transition from the old to the new order was effected without disastrous confusion."[5]

The Preparatory Period

Bellamy, the speculative man who disliked violence,[6] desired a transition to the ideal state that created no bloody conflicts and that was the result of the desire of the people. He had suggested the inadequacy of violence in *The Duke of Stockbridge:* an armed rebellion had occurred, the legislature had passed some inadequate laws to modify the situation, and the rebels were soon again in bondage to the wealthy. Years later Bellamy wrote in the unpublished preface to *Equality* that there had been "innumerable revolutions great and little in human affairs," but they had had "merely superficial" effects because they had "left untouched the fundamental fact on which the social organization through all the mutations of history has continued to stand—that is, the division of mankind into rich and poor, masters and servants, superiors and dependents. Nearly all institutions are either founded on this great underlying fact or have been conformed to it . . . "[7]

Bellamy, the student of history who had read about the French Revolution in Carlyle, Taine, and Hugo,[8] and who had also portrayed the lack of economic equality after the American Revolution, realized in an editorial of 1872 that "in a government like our own, where the people make and unmake constitutions and laws, all just reforms can be effected legally and constitutionally, so soon as the people are convinced that they are just, [and] any attempt to force them by illegal means beyond the convictions of the people, is sure to react against them."[9] As a result of the recognition of the power of the people, of their desire to achieve the ideal state without conflict and destruction, and of the necessity of developing the new state that had aims selected and enforced by the citizens,[10] Bellamy's keys to such accomplishments were education, religion, and political action to assure the eventual development of the ideal state.[11]

Bellamy's early approach to the education of the people had been stated in his articles in the *Springfield Union.* There he had indicated that, when a man was ill and his ordinary habits were disrupted, he was then most likely to change his ways. And he had argued that periods of economic distress that bred discontentment made men seek cures for their social ills.[12] In *Looking Backward* he asserted that the widespread industrial and social ills of the nineteenth century promoted the formation of the new order. The experiences of citizens educated them to the need for change in their social order, and the abuses of individualism had created such economic misery that labor organizations and many different reform groups and leaders caused chaotic situations and, in the process, often educated the people only about specific ills that needed attention. To supply the atmosphere that would promote order from chaos, Bellamy relied upon specific education of the people and upon awakening in them a religious enthusiasm of brotherly love which, together, would show the citizens not only what had to be done but how to do it. Before any Counter Revolution could be successful, the people had to be intellectually, morally, and economically informed and prepared for it (*LB,* 274). The means for such enlightenment were literary works, lectures, and active believers in the cause.

Although Bellamy recognized that labor organizations had been among the first foes of capitalism because they had introduced the first phase of the revolt against the plutocracy, they had not really accomplished anything truly constructive because, like the farmers, they had only sought to ameliorate their own conditions (*LB,* 5–6; *E,* 208–9, 323).[13] The many strikes that had occurred in the 1860s, 1870s, and 1880s had aroused the world to an awareness of the industrial problem and had kept attention upon it. But, because of the failure of the labor groups and the farmers to solve their problems and to get lasting improvements, the general population had become convinced that capitalism could not be resisted, that they could not return to the pre-Civil-War days of free competition, and that another solution had to be found (*E,* 208–9, 332–33).[14]

Like the laborers and the farmers, many shortsighted reformers—the pacifists, the prohibitionists, the suffragettes, the antimonopolists—had expected their specific reforms to resolve all problems; for they had not discovered that the basic cause of the ills of the time was the economic system itself (*E,* 277–78, 324–25, 330). In his writings in the *Springfield Union* during the 1870s Bellamy had criticized the lack of wisdom of reformers who were so vehement, vindictive, slanderous, hypocritical, or sentimental that they alienated the interest of the public and defeated their own causes.[15] In *Looking Backward* Bellamy stated that the anarchists had deprived even the best of the social reformers of a hearing because they had sought to reform through fear and had not realized that the American people had to be won to accept ideas before any progress could be made (*LB,* 10, 215). In his subsequent letters and articles Bellamy evinced his keen awareness of the proper tactics that had to be used to educate and win the people, and he evinced a knowledge of the obstacles that any reform group had to overcome.

To Bellamy, the people who were to be won to a cause had to be treated as gentlemen and as equals. A reformer was not to feel superior to the citizens or denounce them if they did not accept his beliefs; for doing so closed the door upon the opportunity for conversion and also disclosed the reformer's own weakness.[16] Bellamy advised, therefore, that the rich were not to be slandered and that their sins of commission were to be ascribed to the capitalistic system; and he took the same attitude toward the treatment of Christians and their ministers.[17] Bellamy advised the reformers to make their appeals in simple, clear language; to be quiet and straightforward; and to be earnest in manner in order to win the confidence and support of the thinking, law-abiding masses of the American people.[18] If the people were to consider the merits of what was said by the reformer, he had to be a man of education and position as the leaders of 1776 had been; and, to appeal successfully to the audience, his definition of the aims of the proposed reformation had to be simple but inclusive enough to become the common affair of all people.[19] As Bellamy had himself discovered, the two common ends before every man were "to provide for himself, then for his wife and children"; and, to achieve these desired aims, as well as the cooperative state, men had to be taught and shown that they alone could not achieve their personal objectives.[20]

In *Equality* Bellamy warned the reformers that they would not find it easy to reach the public because the newspapers, the ministers, and the teachers were controlled by the capitalists and could not, for the most part, be relied upon for assistance (*E,* 335, 228). Among the other obstacles the reformers had to face when educating the people and persuading them to change the social order were ignorant prejudices, mistaken attitudes, and the inertia created by hopelessness. Before the citizens would be ready intellectually and morally for the introduction of practical steps to achieve the ideal state, they had to be educated away from the idea that man is innately depraved and that his wickedness would make the new order an impossible goal. To counter these views, the reformer had to teach people to regard the human race as innately good and as capable of developing the social, generous instincts it possessed when given a more healthful environment (*E,* 156, 331, 228, 384; *LB,* 230–32).

Because Americans believed in free competition and feared change of any kind, they would have to be taught the value of democracy and then be shown that such competition and their democracy had been destroyed by the plutocracy. After such teaching, they had to be presented with the new state as the restorer of their democratic equalities because it gave them more liberty, more opportunity, more security, and more happiness and fulfillment than had the system of private enterprise (*E,* 9–10, 21–23, 116). The reformers would also have to convince the citizens that there was no reason for poverty to exist in the ideal state, and they had to stress that— if the Counter Revolution were not to be a complete failure— economic equality, as well as political equality, was the fundamental principle upon which the new state would rest.[21]

To prepare the reformers to meet the arguments that the capitalists would present against the ideal state, Bellamy explained that the following arguments of the plutocrats could be easily applied to what they themselves had done or created: that federal capitalism would destroy individuality, originality, independence of thought, and the incentive in men to work; that it would be impossible to find good leaders for such a new state; that the government itself would be corrupt; and that such a government would kill competition and the liberties of men. And, as for the Malthusians, they too were to be shown the fallacies of their arguments (*E,* 402, 382–83).

Bellamy also alerted reformers that they were to favor the increase and the improvement of education, for future citizens had to be prepared in the schools for the roles they would play in the ideal state. Although he also stressed that the people were to be re-educated relative to their social and political views, he did not wish them to adopt new concepts unthinkingly: they had to be capable of independent and clear thinking and of united action not only to achieve the ideal state but to insure its success. Bellamy believed that nothing was to be feared and that much was to be gained by the development of such analytical thought; for he was certain that, when intelligent, serious people considered the merits of his plan, they would become convinced of the necessity of changing the system of private enterprise and of adopting his cooperative society. Indeed, he believed that, until the citizens rationally knew exactly what they desired, the time for the Counter Revolution had not yet come (*E, 384–85*)[22]

However, Bellamy also wished the nation to be prepared emotionally by a Great Revival that would fill the citizens with a religious enthusiasm for brotherly love that would inspire them to free themselves from the bondage of selfishness and enable them to unite in a true fraternity. When men had been taught to no longer despise themselves as depraved, when they had envisioned the world that could be theirs if they had hope and love in their hearts, and when they denounced the anti-Christian individualistic life that had been that of barbarians, their hearts and their imaginations would be captured by the ideal of social, not personal, salvation. With that change they would also accept the possibility of achieving a heaven on earth by applying the Golden Rule of Christ to the economic, social, and political life of the nation (*LB, 229–33; E, 285, 305, 338*).

To Bellamy, the proper preparation for the creation of the ideal state was most important; without it, the economical and political factors would fail to fulfill the aims of creating a state based upon ethical principles, and also fail to equate economic equality with political and social equality.[23] He had written during his career with the *Springfield Union* that men did not accomplish things through laws but through "heart work" and that the world could only be set right by love, belief in God and His goodness, and faith and belief not only in the future but in the power of Christian truth and grace to bring it about.[24] His own beliefs in solidarity and in the universal spirit in man caused him to write in *Equality* that the fundamental doctrine and practice that men had to accept in their hearts and strive to fulfill was that which Christ had stated when "he declared that the Golden rule of equal and best treatment for all was the only right principle upon which people could live together." (*E, 305*).

The Period of Transition

Bellamy's first hint of the specific and practical steps to be taken toward conversion from private to state capitalism was made in a letter of December 1888 to Thomas Wentworth Higginson. Bellamy remarked that Charles Francis Adams's suggestion that the railroads combine in order to escape bankruptcy meant the eventual nationalization not only of these facilities but of the iron and steel industries. Adams's speech, wrote Bellamy, would have made an excellent footnote for *Looking Backward,* because it described the process from corporate to national control.[25] In subsequent speeches and articles Bellamy argued that the procedure was to be one of "progressive nationalization of industry" and that this action would occur on two levels: local and national.[26] The local level would include the municipalization of public service facilities, such as light, heat, water, coal yards, gas plants, ferries, and other transportation systems. The effective working of these publicly owned and controlled operations and their cheaper services would result in good object lessons for the citizens about the benefits of the new order.[27] On the national level nationalization would include all the newly discovered natural resources, the liquor distribution businesses, and the quasi-public services or those involved in interstate commerce, such as the railroads, the telephone, the express service, the coal mines, the iron and steel industries, and the life insurance companies.[28]

Bellamy maintained that these businesses would be the first to be nationalized because they were so directly connected with the welfare of the citizens, because they were so powerful that they interfered with the welfare of the people, and because they were so highly systematized and organized that the government could quickly and easily take control and manage them.[29] The other and more general business of the nation was to be nationalized when either economic difficulties or exploitation of the people warranted such action. The first to be nationalized would obviously be the producers that supplied the people with the necessities of life. But here the procedure of nationalization would be somewhat different, since the government had first to control them and then to assume ownership of them.[30] The last property to be nationalized would be the land, because it was the basis of all property, of banks, and of mortgages; for to nationalize the land first, as Henry George had suggested, would be foolish, since such an action would antagonize too many interests at the beginning of the period of conversion.[31]

In his articles and speeches Bellamy also outlined what would happen to the employees of nationalized businesses: they would be maintained as government employees, and they would serve under a merit system. Any new employees were to be selected by a non-competitive examination, and neither an old nor a new employee would be dismissed from a job without a hearing by the tribunal. Moreover, the government policy would be to create better and safer working conditions, to regulate the hours of labor, to remunerate the employee fairly, and to provide him with pensions and disability insurance. As a result, the security, benefits, health, and happiness of the workers would not only form the nucleus of the future industrial work force but would also provide favorable examples of the benefits of Nationalism.[32]

As for the unemployed, they were to be put to work in government-established shops which would remunerate them with only the necessities of life. As the number of the government employees increased because of the continued nationalization of industries, these shops would serve as a nucleus of the government factories; for they would produce articles to be sold at cost in the government stores to the civil service workers who would pay for them with a special government-issued script.[33] To insure that nationalized industries and shops would have freedom from political interference by management, the leaders of the Counter Revolution were to secure a civil service reform that would kill forever the vicious "spoils system."[34] And, in order to prepare for the ideal state, the revolutionists were also to advocate not only the end of inheritance but also the needed compulsory education of children.[35]

In *Equality* Bellamy added very little to the details of the transition period he had described in his speeches, articles, and *Looking Backward;* but the narrative in his last utopian novel set out the five steps demanded for the formation of the Great Capitalist. First, municipal public services and interstate quasi-public services were nationalized to serve as examples of the benefits of nationalized industries and to permit the formation of the first industrial work force (*E,* 353–54). Second, public service stores (with goods purchased from the capitalists) for government employees were established (*E,* 357, 354–55). To be able to supply these stores, to employ the unemployed, and to put into cultivation the idle land, the government, as the third step, began to farm the land and to run the idle factories. Idle merchant ships and fishing fleets were used by the government for exporting to other countries the excess products of the government's farms and factories, for importing the necessary supplies for the government stores, and for securing the sea foods for the government employees. The government paid the owners of these unprofitable lands, factories, and ships a compensatory income based on the value of the facility being used (*E,* 355, 367–68). During this same period public dining rooms, laundries, and household service agencies were also established for the civil service workers so that women would be enabled to join the industrial work force (*E,* 357–58, 369–70).

Because of the satisfactory life of the civil service workers and because of the immense savings made by them, other citizens were eager to join their work force and share their benefits; and, as a result, the government not only permitted all who so desired to become national employees but also accepted all the land and all the factories from owners who wished to part with their possessions. The use of the government script became so prevalent because of the millions now employed by the government that the fourth step occurred: the financial system collapsed, money lost its value, and all who wished to live had to enter the national service. When all possible resistance had been overcome, the people had become members of the national service; and, when the lands and industries were under national ownership, economic equality was instituted with the sanction of the citizenry; and the fifth and the last step of the Counter Revolution and the transition period had occurred. Economic equality, the "keystone of the arch of the social fabric," was fittingly and necessarily the last item to be inaugurated (*E,* 357–58, 360–61).[36]

Principles and Formation of the Work Force

In order to provide the economic equality upon which the citizens relied, the organization of the labor force of the nation became a necessity. Bellamy made the unfortunate mistake in *Looking Backward* of comparing his state-employed workers with the European universal military service system, which, he admitted, had given him the idea of universal conscription of labor. He had also borrowed from the European military system the principle that the common duty of each citizen was the contribution of his service, as well as the ideas of complete cooperation and of central oversight of the work force. Although such work organizations had already been thought about and even spoken of in terms of an army by Etienne Cabet, François Fourier, and E. E. Hale,[37] Bellamy's critics—William Morris, W. L. Garrison, and General Francis A. Walker[38]—pounced upon the term "industrial army" and charged that his intention was regimentation.

Although Bellamy answered the charges of Morris and others with succinct statements in his articles in the *New Nation* and later in *Equality,* his best answer was the following paragraph:

Always excepting this precious liberty of loafing, I am quite unable to understand what liberties the nationalist plan of industrial organization curtails. Assuming that it is a right to require a man to work, is it a loss of liberty to guarantee him the opportunity to work at what he likes best and can do best? Is it tyranny to insure him promotion, leadership and honor in precise proportion to his achievements? Is it a curtailment of his liberty to make him absolutely free of dependence upon the favor of any individual or community for his livelihood by giving him the constitutional pledge of the nation for it? Is it oppressive to guarantee him against loss of income in old age, and absolute security as to the welfare of his wife and children after he has gone? If to do all these things for a man means to take away his liberties and tyrannize over him, we had better get a new dictionary for the definitions in the old ones are evidently all wrong.[39]

As this statement indicates, Bellamy had given much thought to the organized industrial work force which was to replace the "unscientific manner" in which the nation had produced in the past. He foresaw scientific, concerted action (*LB,* 264) as the means of solving the labor-wage problem, preventing the wastes of private industry, resolving the problem of getting the dirty work done,[40] and providing the national income or resources upon which economic equality would be based.

In *Looking Backward* and in his notebooks Bellamy recorded many reasons that labor was good not only for the body but for the mind. It was beneficent to the development of both the mind and the body; it was the cure for boredom even for those with the best intellects; it was the method by which men could see themselves in something they produced or created and could thereby come to know themselves. Although Bellamy believed that full enjoyment of life could be achieved only if men cultivated and developed all their faculties by employing them in various occupations, he did not desire that men would become so engrossed in their work that they would sacrifice their lives to it. The maxim he wished to emphasize was "we do not live to work but work to live"—and true living meant "to live the fullest, freest, most developed life we can" (*LB*, 210).[41]

In an 1873 editorial in the *Springfield Union*, "Earning before Spending," Bellamy asserted that labor was the debt that every man owed to society and that, to fulfill his obligation, each man had to contribute enough work to "cover his own maintenance and that of those who depended upon him." Here Bellamy also indicated that the man who lived upon inherited wealth was no better than a pauper since he was not earning his own living but was being supported by the labor of others.[42] In the ideal state the principle of enlistment in the labor corps was similar to that of the army: it was the duty of every able-bodied person to contribute to the protection and welfare of the nation before he could devote himself to his higher duty to himself—the exercise of his intellectual and spiritual faculties that was the main business of his existence.[43]

Since all adults worked for the nation and for one another, no stigma was attached to any kind of service, since it was a form of tax levied upon all citizens (*LB*, 126, 71, 47). But, just as the individual had his duty for the good of all and his contract with the state, the state also had its duty—to supply him with the work that was his means of life (*LB*, 71). Before the ideal state developed, mass unemployment had existed because of the innate weaknesses of the capitalistic organizations; but the government of the year 2000 fulfilled its "first and greatest duty" to "guarantee the livelihood of the people."[44] Bellamy publicly supported this view in 1892 in a letter read at a meeting in Boston at which Burgess McLuckie spoke on behalf of the Homestead strikers: "If the capitalists who insist on managing the industries which are the means of livelihood of the people, can guarantee employment on fair terms to all who wish to work, well and good. If they cannot or will not, we must look further. There is no business so properly devolving upon any government which pretends to represent the people, as that of guaranteeing them a livelihood by providing them with work.[45] In the same year Bellamy printed in the *New Nation* news about a resolution adopted by the workingman's party of Switzerland at a convention in Berne that called for an amendment to the constitution which would "guarantee the right to work." Bellamy then proposed that an immediate solution to the problem of unemployment would be for the government to establish industries that would employ the unemployed, distribute the products to the workers who produced them, and thereby institute the right of the government to supply labor—particularly labor in industries that would not compete with privately owned and operated ones.[46]

Although Bellamy had stated in a November 1874 editorial for the *Springfield Union* that it had been the idea of Napoleon III to sponsor great public works in order to provide employment to people, he also stated that the economy of such a project had been recognized by Cornelius Vanderbilt and the Baltimore and Ohio Railroad, which had been able to repair its tracks with cheap labor during the depression. Bellamy supported the concept of government employment of the unemployed by pointing out that the government always had money, that the work that could be provided was not makeshift but necessary, and that, therefore, the work accomplished was not wholly for the benefit of the unemployed citizens.[47] He had had ample opportunity to become acquainted with this method of caring for the unemployed through his knowledge of the ideas of Comte and L. Blanc.[48] He also knew that the mayor of Boston had asked in 1873 that the municipality provide a public building for the employment of the unemployed,[49] and that in 1885, the mayor of Springfield, H. M. Phillips, had introduced a bill in the state legislature which would have permitted the establishment of municipal industries. (Phillip's idea had been opposed by the *Springfield Republican,* as well as by others, because of the fear that it would hurt privately owned industries.)[50] Bellamy had long been acquainted with the Elizabethan law that had required work to be provided for those able and willing to work so that they could live at home, support their families, and enjoy their existence: he had made an entry relative to this law in his notebook about the comments of Blackstone.[51]

Whatever the source of Bellamy's ideas relative to government employment of the unemployed, he was concerned in his journals, in his short stories, and in his editorials with what motivated people in respect to the work they selected; and the thoughts that he expressed in these works were important in *Looking Backward* and in *Equality.* He analyzed in his journals his own desire to be a writer[52] and to achieve fame; in his unpublished essay "The Force of Flattery" he enlarged upon the theme of the power of flattery, noting that man's greatest love was his selfish vanity and self-conceit.[53] More important to the views he was to express in his utopian novels, however, was his recognition that man's search for money was not for the coins themselves but for the "power and consequence" wealth secured, the excitement of its pursuit, and the "enjoyment of the full swing of energies" that made the chase rewarding.[54]

In the short story "Pott's Painless Cure" (1879) Bellamy had discussed the motives of human conduct; he concluded that little needed to be considered "besides personal vanity and love of approbation." Moreover, the greatest deterrent of "exhibitions of unworthiness" was man's fear of the "shocked surprise of others" rather than "their deliberate reprobation."[55] In his editorials about the solution of the industrial problems of his day Bellamy stated that, since man was basically selfish and since there was not time to change him, the solution was to use his selfish interests by turning them into channels that would serve the good of all. In his ideal society Bellamy, who never changed his view that man was naturally selfish and self-conceited, addressed those human needs by providing not only material security but honors, power, and administrative positions for those who had successfully served the public good. Although the workers of the ideal society were not permitted, as has been noted, to accumulate material wealth except for specifically defined purposes, they also had one human appetite to appease: hunger. If they did not work, they would not eat. Besides the desire for physical comfort which their work could provide, their innate talents and interests were satisfied not only by the method to be used for the selection of their work but also by their working conditions and hours of labor.

The highest motives that were to spur men to zealous labor included not only interest in the work itself but an ethical sense of duty, the public spirit created by the brotherhood of man, and an enthusiasm for humanity that was to be similar to that inspired by patriotism in time of war (LB, 73–74, 76).[56] Just as the centripetal force made man selfish and self-conceited, the centrifugal force in him would encourage not only his devotion to the welfare of others but also his desire to submerge self in religion, in love of work, and in all deeds of self-sacrifice and heroism.[57] To Bellamy, this impersonal side of man was his noblest; such men needed no models to spur them to action since their motives were within; and they knew that their measure of service to society was established by their natural endowments. To these servitors of mankind, emulation seemed "philosophically absurd" and "despicable in a moral aspect by its substitution of envy for admiration, and exultation for regret, in one's attitudes toward the successes and failures of others" (*LB*, 103). But, since all men were not of this high caliber, emulation was adopted to supply motivation for the inferior natures. Bellamy hoped, of course, that such motivation would be unnecessary in future ages.

In the meantime, he recognized that, for most people, to destroy competition would also be to ignore human nature;[58] and he defended the use of competition by indicating that the struggle was made truly just by providing for all citizens an equal opportunity for education, equal opportunities to work, equal remuneration, and a relatively equal recognition of merit (*LB*, 74–75, 101; *E*, 394–98).[59] As a result, rewards for accomplishments resulted from competition in the schools and in the industrial army;[60] and those who were most successful were given their preference relative to jobs:[61] they gained higher grades or rank within the industrial work force,[62] they were given official positions,[63] and they received awards and publicity (*LB*, 74–75).

The realistic Bellamy also provided for the citizens who would not react favorably either to inferior or to superior motivations: he recommended indirect and direct discipline. Indirect discipline was to be issued by men and women whose welfare depended upon the contribution of all the citizens of the ideal state, for their attitudes toward the malingerer would be ones of such disapproval that the person would strive to avoid such public contempt.[64] Women were, however, to express their disapproval of the nonworkers by denying them their love: Bellamy pictured the females as sitting aloft as judges of the race and as reserving themselves as rewards for the distinguished worker (*LB*, 215). (In this view of women he seemingly overlooked the fact that some women might also be malingerers that the successful workers might not desire and that such females might be pleased to accept the attention of a slacker!)

To insure that every person would contribute to the welfare of the nation by working, Bellamy indicated in *Looking Backward* that, if a man did not contribute his share to the maintenance of society, he automatically severed his relationship with it (*LB*, 47); for, if he refused to work, he would be sentenced to solitary confinement with a diet of bread and water until he was willing to accept his duty to the society of the whole (*LB*, 101, 168). In his later articles Bellamy repeated that the man who refused to work would be institutionalized and made to work under disciplinary conditions prepared for such individuals.[65] Since the best-qualified men were to be officials and since the inspectorate could trace any faulty article back to the workman,[66] Bellamy said that the discipline of the officials of industry would be too strict to permit neglect of work or positively bad work by either the inefficient or the malingering worker. As a result, inefficiency would result in demotion or in being given longer working hours or harder tasks to perform; but, to protect such workers, he provided that a tribunal of the people judge each case so that the judgment of the officials under whom the man worked would not fully determine his fate.[67]

Mrs. Frances E. Russell suggested in 1893 to Bellamy that he replace solitary confinement by permitting the rebels to go "off upon land not actually in use by the commonwealth and there try the experiment of individualism to their heart's content"; for this type of life would soon make them desire the freedom that association in labor gave them.[88] In *Equality* Bellamy made no mention of his former suggestion about corporal punishment; instead, he stated that those unwilling to work would be given tools and seeds and be permitted to withdraw to reservations that would be similar to those of the Indians; there they would have to discover their own solutions to the problems of existence (*E*, 41).

Bellamy may also have listened to women in developing the plans he had outlined in *Looking Backward* for the formation of the industrial armies of workers, since he had outlined in this novel the men's army and its three allied corps: the women's army, the invalid's, and the professional's. To Bellamy, the army of females was necessary because of the "conditions of . . . sex";[69] for he still held the views he had expressed in 1875 in the *Springfield Union* about the role of women as workers. He had discussed two views of the enfranchisement of women: that of the suffragettes who demanded complete economic independence for women and also equality of the right to work; and that of the counter-movement—led by Maudsley, Van de Worker, and Clark—which maintained that the ability of women to be independent and to work was limited by their physical and mental weaknesses. In the same article, Bellamy cited in the *Union* that Azel Ames in *Sex in Industry* had written that the effect of industrial work upon women's health was permanently injurious and that women should work "only under conditions especially adapted to their needs, and involving an elastic arrangement allowing short periodical vacations and long annual vacations."

In *Looking Backward* Bellamy effected a compromise by giving women the complete economic independence from their husbands that the suffragettes wanted and by assigning them the lighter tasks—because of their "comparative weakness and uncertainty of their health"—demanded by the anti-suffragettes. Although the women could select their tasks according to their innate abilities, they could not pursue any line of work not "completely adapted both as to kind and degree of labor, to . . . [their] sex"; and they were given shorter working hours, more frequent vacations, and more frequent daily rest periods. Since Bellamy also recognized not only the distinct physical needs of women but also "the distinct individuality of the sex," he placed them in a separate industrial army which avoided "unnatural rivalry with men" and permitted the women to have their own ambitions, desires, careers, and emulation (*LB*, 210–11).

In an April 1891 essay in the *New Nation* Bellamy stated a very different approach: all women who were mentally and physically capable would be required to do whatever work they elected to do and could prove themselves capable of doing.[70] In *Equality* he made no mention of the separate industrial army for women; instead, they were portrayed as taking their places in the industrial state on the same basis as men (*E*, 268) and as being superintendents of plants, machinists, carpenters, iron workers, builders, and farm laborers (*E*, 43–44). Although he knew that Gronlund had also provided labor that was appropriate for the physical and mental differences of women, and that John Stuart Mill had advocated that all employment be open to women, Bellamy based his position on the reaction of women to his separate army.[71] Mrs. Abby Morton Diaz and Mary H. Ford expressed in their articles acute displeasure with the restrictions Bellamy placed upon women: like Mary Livermore, they felt that the sphere of labor of females was to be limited only by the training they had, and they also maintained that women were to be trained for any work they could do.[72]

Since Bellamy believed that physical defects did not render a person totally incapable of labor, he created the invalid's industrial army. Bellamy had noted in the *Springfield Union* in 1873 that not infrequently "the most attractive and salable articles" at a benevolent fair had been those produced by invalids.[73] In *Looking Backward* the invalid corps provided the deaf, the mute, the insane, the blind, and the crippled with tasks fitted to their ability and strength; even the completely disabled individual who could not work at all continued to receive his full income because he was a human being (*LB*, 104–5; *E*, 97). Aside from such statements relative to the invalid corps, Bellamy did not present any other information about its management, its relationship with production groups, or its means of distribution.

The professional army was to be made up of teachers, authors, artists, and physicians who had been released from the industrial army when they had proved their original genius and had paid for the privilege of doing so, or when they had successfully fulfilled their professional requirements and training (*LB*, 156, 131–32). The members of the technical professions (architects and engineers) formed part of the construction guilds—and were therefore members of a special unit of the industrial army (*LB*, 156). As for the legal and religious professions, they did not exist in the year 2000; for Bellamy, like James Fenimore Cooper in *The Crater* and Melville in *Typee*, regarded these professions as sources of trouble and as not contributing to the harmony, solidarity, and serenity of life. Because Bellamy had realized that the natural aptitudes of a person were often late in developing (*LB*, 55–56, 155–57), he stipulated that a person might become an artist or an author any time in his life; but he restricted the right to select either the medical or the engineering profession to before the citizen was thirty.

Bellamy reflected in *Equality* the attitudes toward the medical profession that he had expressed in the *Springfield Union* in the 1870s. There he had lambasted the deficiencies of the physicians and of the medical schools of his own country.[74] The medical profession of his ideal state was not only well trained but had to pass severe examinations before being permitted to practice (*LB*, 96; *E*, 283). Since the economic income of the doctors was no longer endangered by medical progress which might make their sectarian practices obsolete, the doctors encouraged medical research and the adoption of new ideas (*E*, 283–84, 228–29). As Bellamy had advocated in the *Springfield Union*, the public in *Equality* had become so well educated in medical science that a citizen merely consulted a physician relative to his own diagnosis and treatment (*E*, 184). The citizen had the right to select the doctor of his choice. The doctor was paid by deducting the cost of the visit and/or treatment from the patient's credit fund—an amount that the doctor had, however, to submit to the nation, which also established the price for all ailments and treatments (*LB, 96*).

To be certain that all individuals developed their innate abilities and were placed in the proper work corps, Bellamy stressed that the educational system and three years of service in the general work corps of the industrial army were to be preparations for the proper development and placement of all citizens. By the age of twenty-one—when they entered the general work group—the citizens had attended the community universities and had also been educated by technological devices. But, as Bellamy made clear in *Equality*, the best time for the development of many branches of learning came after twenty-one, since youth was not "the time of life for ardent and effective study" (*E, 249*). As the youthful citizens did their stint in the general work corps, their leaders observed and studied their abilities in order to give them work assignments that would enable them to become acquainted with the appropriate trade or profession (*LB, 49–50*). Each worker was, however, to develop his multiple abilities as much as possible so that he would be capable of adapting to different types of work. Bellamy sponsored such preparation in *Looking Backward* because he argued that the government might have to shift a citizen to a vacant position, might not be able to place him if no vacancy existed in his favorite work, or could no longer place him because his job had become obsolete through invention or technological development (*LB, 52, 99*).

Bellamy also stipulated in *Looking Backward* that the final placement of the worker depended upon his ability and his service record while doing general work, for preference was to be given to those with the highest grades and the greatest ability. After their three-year term had ended and their abilities had been determined, their training for their specific work assignments or professions began. As for the individuals who had no specific choice of work or no specific talents, they remained in the general work corps until their retirement; and this group performed the work that had so concerned Bellamy—the dirty work of the nation (*LB, 49–57, 97–109*). To supply the other needs of the nation, work that was particularly dangerous was made attractive to young men who were greedy for honor by the government's announcing that they deserved public gratitude for their performance (*LB, 51*). If, however, a shortage of volunteers occurred, the government could draft men to do the work or the administration could so modify the hours or conditions that some citizens would select it as their permanent occupation (*LB, 51*).

In *Looking Backward* Bellamy had stated that it was possible for men to change their occupations as well as the locations in which they worked (*LB, 54*); but in *Equality* he systematized his plan of selection and location by establishing the labor exchange, which he had first mentioned in his article " 'Looking Backward' Again."[75] As Cabet had suggested,[76] the Bellamy government of *Equality* published a statement that indicated the workers required in all areas of industry; and each graduate of the general work corps not only studied the positions available but also stated his preferences not only for the work he wished but the location of it. Then the local registrar identified the merit rating the applicant had achieved during his education and his work career. This rating denoted his relative intelligence, his devotion to duty, and his efficiency. This record eventually determined the work assignment that the government would give him.

After the local exchange had completed and stamped the citizen's application, it was sent to the central office of the industrial district, which allocated assignments according to the rank of all those requesting work either in their home area or outside it. However, if the applicant's ranking and the work desired did not correlate, or if the job was not available, the citizen was assigned to an available position in his native locality. Applications that had expressed no desire for a location in the home territory were sent to the national board, which made assignments according not only to the person's rank and preferences, but also to the national need. By the first of August each applicant was notified of his job assignment; and he reported for service on Muster Day, 15 October.

During the years of service in the industrial army or the professions, which lasted until the individual reached the age of forty-five, the administration, which sought earnestly to supply the needs of each citizen, gave special consideration through the attention of the transfer department to these who were dissatisfied with either their location or their assigned positions. This bureau, which Bellamy described in *Equality* (*E, 36–39*), made it possible for all those who desired to change their work or their location to communicate with one another and to arrange exchanges that would be mutually agreeable. As this plan and others indicated, Bellamy organized his industrial army so that the workers, happy with their selected tasks, would work harder at them; thus the efficiency of their work would lead to their recognition, honors, and promotions by the administration that was comprised of individuals who had been among the outstanding workers and leaders of their own day.

The Administration

The central government described in *Looking Backward* remained relatively unchanged in *Equality*. This lack of alteration of a system that was far from being perfected probably resulted from the author's view of the insignificance of such details relative to a government that would have to be created to fulfill the needs and desires of the era in which it would be developed. As has been noted, Bellamy had alway been as a young man and then as a writer for the *Springfield Union* quite outspoken about the corruption of the political and economic systems and about the destruction of democracy by the plutocracy—a plutocracy that made the voting rights of the citizens ineffective and therefore useless in regard to their welfare.

In 1867, when he was seventeen years old, Bellamy had recorded in his notebook the necessity of reforming the method of selecting the president of the United States in order to insure the achievement of the will of the majority. Under the electoral system, wrote young Bellamy, the electoral votes of each state were cast in accordance with the desire of the party that had the majority of votes; and the voice of what might be the majority of the nation was lost. Although Bellamy advocated in this instance a direct ballot of all citizens,[77] he later considered in the same notebook the problem of equal suffrage among men and decided that his zeal had outrun his reason when he had bestowed the privilege of voting on all. Manhood alone, he wrote, was not a sufficient qualification for exercising the right to vote: a degree of intelligence and information should also be required. Although the requirements were not to be so high that they could not be required in all citizens, he did list one that was to be mandated—literacy.[78]

In the many editorials that he wrote in the 1870s about the elections Bellamy had much to say about the elective and party systems.[79] Elections, he wrote, seemed a "wearisome vanity, . . . a delusion and a snare"; and, because of the din of arguments, the mudslinging, and the profanity of the pre-election period, one felt that the electoral franchise was anything but a blessing. Bellamy admitted, however, that, to the young, the elections were stimulating; to the older cultivated citizens, they were promoters of "common intense interest" and mental stimulation; and, according to each group's capacity, each was touched "with something of the ennobling feeling of belonging to a great brotherhood of men and a vast commonwealth of interests, and [elections gave] to each at least some inkling of what it is to think and act from broad and imperial views of the general good."[81]

In another of his *Union* articles, "Morality and Politics," Bellamy denounced the avarice and the bribery that delivered the country into the hands of unprincipled officials; and he attributed to the influence of the political party part of the lack of personal morality and ethics:

. . . in politics the simplicity of moral issues is disturbed by more numerous, subtle and varied causes. In the first place by merging himself in his party, the citizen to some extent loses his individual conscience, and is actuated only by a sort of corporate public conscience, a much less delicate and reliable standard. Moreover, he is carried away by the tumultuous influence of a great multitude. The low principles of political action are derived from the traditions of dissimulation as formerly produced in diplomacy in an age when diplomats boasted of their cunning and triumphs by the use of the basest means of briberty and deceit.[82]

In other articles published in the *Springfield Union* in the 1870s Bellamy stated that the dissimulation practiced by the parties and by their leaders led to lying to the public, to slandering and personal abuse of men,[83] to fooling the public about the freedom of democratic discussion within the parties themselves,[84] and to killing such progressive movements as civil-service reform which would be destructive to the parties' patronage systems.[85] In order to win elections, the parties resorted to buying votes and to stuffing the ballot boxes; and he cited an example: two leaders of the Molly Maguires had been paid a thousand dollars each to turn over the votes of their organization to the party.[86] Moreover, a news story, "Bribery in New York," printed in 1880 in the *Daily News,* related the selling of votes for twenty and fifty dollars; and the newspaper also reported that four hundred men in one large factory had been given three dollars each for casting their votes for a certain presidential candidate.[89]

When Julian West discusses with Dr. Leete in *Looking Backward* the administrators of the industrial army, West is told that, because of the various and severe tests of their abilities, there could be little doubt about their administrative abilities; for the "social system leaves them absolutely without any other motive than that of winning the esteem of their fellow citizens. Corruption is impossible in a society where there is neither poverty to be bribed nor wealth to bribe, while as to demagoguery or intrigue for office, the conditions of promotion render them out of the question" (*LB*, 156). Although Bellamy described the administration of the new government as having evolved from the former one upon lines that were easily detected as existing,[88] he seemingly had two sources for his germinal ideas about the administrative branch of his government: the general staff of a great European army and the social-service regulations that existed in Sweden and in England.

In 1876 in the *Springfield Union* Bellamy had published his views about the civil-service reform movement in "A Reform Worth Having." The cabinet of the president would consist of members of the Senate and of the House of Representatives, since this change would lessen the appointive powers of the chief executive, make his cabinet members more responsible to the party for what they did, and also give them power to secure the legislation that was needed. As for subordinate officials, they were to be selected because of their ability and retained only because of their efficiency. Bellamy's intention was, he stated, to secure less "personal government" and to insure that the administration would be sustained by measures and not by men.[89]

When Bellamy summarized in 1877 in an editorial in the *Union* a paper entitled "Swedish Civil Service," he noted that civil service in Sweden was based upon educational requirements: all lesser officials had to have a high school education, and those of higher rank had to pass university examinations of a non-competitive nature. The appointive powers of the king were limited to officials who were to have only confidential duties, and no political considerations influenced other appointments since ability and merit alone secured both employment and advancement. Moreover, no members of the civil service could be removed except by judicial trial. These officials were, Bellamy noted, "regarded precisely as officers of the Army are in America."[90]

In 1890 in "What 'Nationalism' Means" Bellamy wrote that the administration he had depicted in *Looking Backward* compared to the "offices of the general staff of one of the great European armies" with its departments of paymaster-general, commissariat, transportation, engineering and construction, ordnance and war material, as well as its various government manufacturing establishments that supplied the army. The general staff had facilities that enabled it to know all the resources of the country, and of it Bellamy wrote:

. . . the business of organizing and fully providing for all the needs of a body of men comprising the whole early manhood of a nation, including machinery for utilizing the entire material resources of the country in the case of need, involves the constant solution of problems of business administration on a far greater scale than they are presented by the affairs of the largest industrial or commercial syndicates, and that, as a matter of fact, the work of the epauletted administrators is done with an exactitude and fidelity unequalled in private business. Upon this administrative and essentially business side of the great modern military organizations the advocate of the practicability of Nationalism may properly lay peculiar stress.[91]

In this same article Bellamy described the administrative officers of his ideal state as having the same sense of duty and the same desire for honor, rank, and power that the soldiers had; but they could not seek financial gain because of economic equality. In another article in which he described the division of powers, he insisted that all members of the different armies would rise to positions of power only as a result of their past and present records of merit and efficiency.[92]

In *Looking Backward* Bellamy presented the organization of the ideal state; he made very little change in it in *Equality;* instead, he devoted more space to the political and economic chicanery that had turned a democracy into a plutocracy. The president of the ideal state was to be the general-in-chief, or the commander-in-chief, of the industrial army, the disciplinarian, and the enforcer of the laws of the republic (*LB,* 152, 155, 157). No member of the professions could qualify for the presidency because the president was required to have risen through the labor and official ranks of the industrial army before becoming the chief of a department; thus his career would have proved that he merited the presidency. After retiring from the industrial forces and after having had his final report approved by the Congress, the potential candidate for the presidency had to spend five years after retirement as a citizen before he could be elected to office; and this specification was made to insure that he would identify himself not with his former department of the industrial army but with the needs of all departments, the populace, and the allied professional, female, and invalid armies (*LB,* 112–13, 153–56).

Because the president was the disciplinarian of the industrial army and because he served as the honorary chairman of the professional army, he was elected by the vote of all the men of the nation who were no longer in active service as industrial workers and by those still in active service in the professional groups. To insure that the president would serve for the benefit of the nation and that he would not be propitiating any group to secure reappointment, Bellamy limited his term to five years. When his term was completed, Congress convened to receive his report; and, if it was approved, he was appointed by Congress to represent the nation on the International Council, a federation of autonomous nations which regulated international commerce (*LB,* 112, 114, 155–56).

As Bellamy had suggested in his article in the *Union* and as he made clear in *Looking Backward,* he limited the appointive powers of the president to that of the judges (*LB,* 166); the members of his Council, which replaced the Cabinet, were elected by the retired members of the ten departments (or guilds) of the industrial forces which each of the candidates had served in different executive offices. Although Bellamy neglected to state how the members of the Inspectorate received their positions, he made it clear not only that all the allied armies had comparable organizations and procedures but that the members of the Inspectorate acted as the right hand of the president in maintaining discipline. Its task was to receive and investigate all complaints about imperfect production, about the insolence or inefficiency of officials, and about the dereliction of workers. The inspectors did not wait, however, for complaints to be filed: they were to conduct methodical inspections of all branches of the service in order to discover what was wrong before anyone else did (*LB,* 155).

The Council of the president consisted of the heads (lieutenant-commanders) of each of the ten departments of the industrial army and also of the woman who was the general-in-chief of the female army; but she could vote only about matters that concerned her corps. Although Bellamy provided on the Council no representation of the invalid corps or of the professional group, the president was the ex-officio chairman of the board of regents of the professional faculties of medicine and education and had "the casting vote" (*LB,* 157). The regents were responsible to Congress, and they had been chosen by the retired members of the guilds of education and medicine.

In the industrial army the heads of the departments (lieutenant-commanders) were required to have risen through all the lower ranks of the laborers and through all the offices of the industrial army—assistant foreman (lieutenant), foreman (captain), colonel (superintendent)—before being elected by the retired members of the departments they had to administer. Each of the ten heads of departments represented on the Council was related to productive or constructive industries which had their own separate but allied bureaus or industries which were commanded by generals of the guilds. The generals had been superintendents (colonels) and had also served as foremen and as assistant foremen after having risen through three ranks in the industrial army.

The generals of the guilds had complete control of all the subordinate industries which might comprise one bureau or many, and they were responsible for all work to the administration. Because of his responsibilities, the general had the complete record of plants and forces under his control, since he had to know the means and capacity of production, for he was responsible for fulfilling the orders relative to production that were sent to him by his department chief. Unlike even the president, the generals had broader appointive power: they chose from the candidates with the best records their superintendents and their other officials. However, the general of the guild was himself elected by the retired members of the guild from among the superintendents (*LB,* 153).

As Dr. Leete makes clear to Julian West in *Looking Backward,* the fact that each guild had its general elected by its retired members was very important; for "no previous form of society could have developed a body of electors so ideally adapted to their office, as regards absolute impartiality, knowledge of the special qualifications and records of candidates, solicitude for the best result, and complete absence of self-interest" (*LB,* 154). Since the retired guild members had their social clubs and were interested in their own welfare, which was in the hands of their successors, "the young aspirants for guild leadership who . . . [could] pass the criticism of . . . [the] old fellows [were] likely to be pretty well equipped" (*LB*, 154). If Dr. Leete takes his own statement seriously, he should have revised his view that the retired electors had "complete absence of self-interest," or he should have made clear that the still-employed laborers in the guilds could not use their power as electors to gain advancement.

The production for which the generals of the guilds were responsible was determined by statistics provided by the department of distribution at the end of each year after the figures had been adjusted to allow for the increase or the decrease in the demand for specific items. After these estimates had been approved by the general administration, the estimates for the forthcoming year were forwarded to the related heads of departments and were considered as mandates. Nonetheless, the department chief and the general administration did not ignore overseeing that the responsible bureau fulfilled its order of goods. Moreover, the materials produced were also investigated by the distributive department as well as by the consumer, and unsatisfactory products were traced to the original workman (*LB*, 148). After the industrial army had assessed its needs relative to production by the workers, those who were not to be employed were used to create "fixed capital, such as buildings, machinery, engineering works, and so forth" (LB, 148).

Despite the studies made by the distributive department of the amount of products needed, those for which no wide demand existed could be produced if the consumer would continue to pay for the desired article; for "the administration has no power to stop the production of any commodity for which there continues to be a demand" (*LB*, 149). Although the cost of the rare product was increased when its scarcity was temporary, or was higher when the insufficiency was permanent, the consumer had the means of paying for it if he wished to sacrifice for it the deduction made from the funds allotted him by economic equality (*LB*, 151). To insure availability of the "great staples of life," a large surplus was always maintained to meet demand or to maintain supply when poor crops occurred.

The government's charge for products sold to the consumer was based upon the cost of production and distribution; but, unlike the employees of the producer and the distributors of the capitalist system, the consumer-producer population all earned an equal amount whether the individual worked four hours a day at hazardous tasks or eight hours in the regular labor forces. As a result, the cost of the laborer in the bureau affected the cost of the product and its price just as the different wages of the nineteenth-century workers had done. As Dr. Leete indicates to Julian West, the competitive capitalists had a lot more to worry about than the president and his Council who "direct the industries of the entire nation . . . and do things the right way [rather] than the wrong. It is easier for a general up in a balloon, with perfect survey of the field, to manoevre a million men to victory than for a sergeant to manage a platoon in a thicket" (*LB,* 152).

Just as the system of production had been simplified, so had that of distribution; for the ideal society had decreased the cost of distribution from one-third to one-half of what it had cost the capitalists, who had had to defray the expenses for rent, salesmen, advertisement, transportation, and accountants. Moreover, since not only production but distribution was "held in trust by the nation for the people," the government also organized distribution in a scientific way and prevented corrupt business practices such as the adulteration of products (*LB,* 66–67). Since all distribution was made without profit to any producer or salesman, the ethical result was a benefit to society; for men in the distributive system no longer had to lie, cheat, or tempt the consumer to buy their products in order to have an income.

Besides the ethical benefits of the distributive system, the physical facilities were centralized and modernized. All the products of the nation went to warehouses centrally located in districts, they were displayed in government-owned stores, and they were delivered to the purchasers by the government's delivery service. Samples of all products were displayed in the stores, where the customers could examine them and read the labels which specified the price, the materials used, and the durability of the item. Clerks merely took and recorded the orders, made the charges against the customer's credit (his income), and then sent the orders in a dispatch box by way of the pneumatic tube which connected the department in the store with the appropriate part of the warehouse. The purchases were then sent by other pneumatic tubes to the city or country district in which the purchaser lived. By the time the city shopper returned to his home, the products he had purchased had already been delivered; even the rural delivery was made rapidly, since the sample store and the warehouse were usually only about twenty miles from the purchasers (*LB,* 84–85).

Although Bellamy provided for the delivery of products to the farmers, he had very little to say about them in *Looking Backward;* but he did discuss in *Equality* the effects of Nationalism upon their work and their lives—and he without doubt did so because of their support of his concepts as members of the People's Party. Despite the delay in giving attention to the sorry plight of the farm population, his articles in the *Springfield Union* in the 1870s and in the *New Nation* in the 1890s indicate that he had observed the agrarian movements against the monopolies, the plight of the English farmer, scientific experiments to improve production but conserve the soil, and the need to make farm life in the isolated areas more attractive.[93] And, as has been observed, he had portrayed in *The Duke of Stockbridge* the plight of the farmers who suffered from foreclosed mortgages, from currency manipulations, and from low prices for their products. In his articles in the *New Nation* Bellamy reported that the American farmer was rapidly becoming a peasant; for, in Kansas and in Ohio, thirty-three percent and thirty-seven percent, respectively, of the landowners had already become peasants. These factors, largely the result of mortgages and foreclosures, explained the revolutionary attitude of the farmers, an attitude that permitted Bellamy to state in 1891 that the Western farmers, "especially those of Kansas and Nebraska," were largely Nationalists.[94]

He attributed the ageless, depressed condition of the farmers to their lack of educational and social facilities such as libraries and theaters; to their geographic isolation, which made political collaboration almost impossible; to their inability to control their hours of work, since nature was their taskmaster; and to the fact that accidents of nature controlled their productivity.[95] He felt the farmer of the 1890s was a small capitalist caught in the economic waste and general disadvantages that had been overcome by businesses conducted on a large scale by consolidated capital. For this reason, Bellamy wrote, neither cheaper railroad nor interest rates would permanently help the farmer; and, since only syndication or Nationalism could solve his problems, Bellamy feared that the former method would only substitute group selfishness for individual selfishness.[96] In "Talks on Nationalism" and in *Equality* he indicated that the two American groups most likely to be helped by Nationalism were the farmers and women.[97]

In *Equality* Bellamy incorporated ideas of the cause of the farmer's plight that he had expressed in the *New Nation*, as well as some of the suggestions about the way their sorry state could be alleviated. The unequal burden of labor that made the farmer's life so disagreeable and that caused his movement to the cities would be equalized by shorter hours for each man, since relays of workers could be shifted from one region to another to perform the seasonal labor (*E*, 304). Since state capitalism would utilize the machinery that had been used on the large bonanza farms, and since its use would not bring ruin to the individual farmer by the production of bumper crops that would cut the market price to below the cost of production (*E*, 241), a scientific and industrial revolution would occur in farming methods. Among such developments would be electric machinery that would make farming so easy that women could do it; railroad lines built on the large collective farms to haul produce to factories and warehouses; the application of scientific methods to install drainage ditches, to plow the land to keep it in good condition, and to fertilize it with the proper mixture of chemicals (*E*, 300). In Bellamy's picture of the intensive culture that was used in the greenhouses to provide vegetables for the winter market, he suggested that hydroponic methods had been introduced (*E*, 301)— and he would have been intrigued by the exhibit of such growth of vegetation by the farm in the Kraft annex at the Epcot Center.

Farming, the basic and essential industry of the nation (*E*, 303), would also become more attractive for the agriculturists because they would no longer live in isolation but in centrally located villages from which they could commute to work and in which they would enjoy the social and cultural advantages that they had not before enjoyed (*E*, 302). Moreover, the radio ("the telephone") and television ("the electroscope") would bring the culture and the entertainment of the nation into their homes, just as they did to Dr. Leete's. Far greater than these advantages in their effect upon the dignity, happiness, and security of the farmer were not only state capitalism's economic equality but also its management of his farms, releasing him from slavery to a mortgage holder, from the speculation of the middle man and other speculators, and from his dependence upon nature for his living and financial welfare (*E*, 96–97, 303, 312–13).[98] The farmer was not the only one to profit from the operation of the collective farms by the government: the general public too would benefit from larger crops and lower prices.

International Trade, Travel, Government

Because some products needed by the nation could not be produced in the United States, Bellamy described in *Looking Backward* how the great countries of the world—those of Europe, as well as Mexico, Australia, and parts of South America—had followed the leadership of his country in becoming industrially organized and by having an International Council and "a loose form of federal union of world-wide extent" (*LB*, 111–12). The International Council not only regulated the commerce and the communication among the countries of the union but also established the policy to be taken by all its member nations toward those backward countries that had not, as yet, been sufficiently educated to become "civilized institutions" (*LB*, 112). Each country's bureau of foreign exchange in turn had to manage the importation and exportation of products. Among this bureau's duties were the estimating of the amount of any product needed; the sending of the orders to the other countries; and the notifying of other countries of any changes made in the products usually exported to them (*LB*, 113). The bureau of foreign trade also had to determine whether or not the materials or products to be imported were requisite for the general welfare of the nation, for Bellamy had cited this need as the basic principle relative to imports (*LB*, 112).

The cost of all the commodities that were traded was established in the same way and at the same price that the American ideal state had established as cost for its citizens; and no nation was permitted to remain in the union if it tried to create a monopoly with its natural resource or its products and thereby extort a profit from other nations (*LB*, 113). Although a guarantee existed relative to the price charged not only to the citizens of a nation but also to a foreign purchaser, such a sharp practice for profit could not have been implemented because of the sense of community that had developed, because of the "conviction of the folly of selfishness" that prevailed, and because of the international expectation of "an eventual unification of the world as one nation . . . the ultimate form of society . . . [that would] realize certain economic advantages over the . . . federal system of autonomous nations" (*LB*, 114).

As a result of the progress that had been made in and among nations, international trade was conducted without money, without custom duties, but with "a simple system of book accounts" (*LB*, 111) that had to be examined at the end of each year for the settlements to be made by the International Council. The balance due a nation by another country was to be settled with staples or other products that were agreed upon by each country before international trade had begun. However, the amounts due to one nation by another could be settled by an exchange of products: one could trade wheat, for example, for what was owed it by a second nation in settlement for what it owed a third nation for leather. Although the balances due did not have to be settled every year, the International Council did require that settlements be made every few years; but, if the amount that was due became too large, the Council had the right to request a debt payment at any time because it did not want "feelings unfavorable to amity" to be developed (*LB*, 114-15).

In *Equality* Bellamy expanded his statements about foreign trade in order to show (1) the reasons for its decrease in the year 2000, (2) the fallacies of the nineteenth century theory that such trade brought general prosperity, (3) the possibility and threat of an international plutocratic regime because of the wealth and power of the merchant princes, and (4) the possibilities in the year 2000 that the International Council would become a world government. When foreign trade ceased to be profitable for the capitalists because of the national ownership of all production and distribution, the desire of every country was to be as self-sufficient as possible. Because of the equalization not only of education and culture but of the knowledge of science and the mechanical arts, each country was much more capable of developing its industries and its natural resources. Moreover, diversified industry was considered beneficial because it made available a variety of jobs and mind-awakening opportunities for the citizens. As a result, the principle of each country was that it would trade with other nations only for the products that it could not produce and that were essential to its citizenry (*E*, 289).

During the nineteenth century private industries had conducted foreign trade for profit with the backward countries and colonies; and they had maintained that foreign trade brought prosperity to their own countries and that it was the result of the natural differences of resources and of cultural developments (*E*, 212–13). To Bellamy, foreign markets were an enrichment for only the few who were unloading shoes and clothing upon the natives of Africa, Asia, and other areas.[99] He argued in *Equality* that the condition of the people who produced the exported wares was worse than it had been before foreign trade began because the competition among countries forced wages down to the level of the industrial country that had the lowest standard of living (*E*, 214–16). Furthermore, both the farmer and the factory worker became dependent on the "delicate balance of a complex set of international adjustments"; their living standards were no longer wholly dependent upon their local situations; they were affected either by those of other countries or by their own catastrophes. (*E*, 217).

Because the capitalists, the merchant princes, had the power through their large-scale production to crush the enterprises of the beginning and weaker industrialists, such industries were not developed in another country; and that country became not only dependent upon the produce of another nation but also the victim of the terms of trade that the capitalists wished to impose (*E*, 216)—a situation, said Bellamy, that had caused the American Revolution (*E*, 217). The notion of free trade and protective tariff meant nothing to the common people, for free trade was advocated by the industrialist powerful enough to enter the world market without fear of the competition of others. As for protective tariff, it was advocated by the weak and beginning industrialist who wished to build a protective wall around his country that would give his business a chance to develop. For the people, the trade conducted by private enterprise meant exploitation by either their own capitalists or by foreign ones; for no one group of merchant princes could be considered more considerate than any other. Because of the wealth and power that the world traders had accumulated, the powerful capitalists threatened to establish a world plutocratic empire that would be more powerful than any envisioned by Napoleon or by Alexander the Great (*E*, 216–21).

To correct and prevent the evils of international trade, the International Council Bellamy had introduced in *Looking Backward* as having no power or right to interfere with the internal affairs of a nation (*LB*, 114–16)[100] became in *Equality* a world union that brought about world peace, ended the economic strife which had been more dangerous than wars, and stopped the jealousies and animosities which had embittered one nation against another. Such unity and understanding were the result of economic equality, state and international control of industry and trade, fraternal sympathy and understanding, and mutual goodwill (*E,* 276–78). To facilitate communication, many countries of the federal union had not only their own language but also a universal one that all people spoke; and many small nations had adopted as their only means of communication the general or universal language (*E,* 257).

Bellamy's dream of one world was an old one not only in classical literature but in the United States, where such thinkers as Thomas Paine and Joel Barlow, as well as the incomparable Victoria Woodhull, had sponsored such a union.[101] In the 1870s Bellamy had stated that he did not base his "faith in the good time coming," the federation of the world, upon the "mystical hyperbole of Jewish seers" or upon any "subjective transcendental philosphies," but upon deductions from undoubted facts.[102] To him, many of the divisive problems of the age, intense prejudices and lack of mutual understanding, were due to the lack of facilities for communication. Modern inventions such as telegraph, newspapers, steamships, and railroads brought countries closer together; and the commerce that existed among them had developed the "closest relations of mutual interest." Because of the intercourse among nations made possible by these inventions, ignorance was being dissipated about the mores and habits of other nations; and, as a result of such studies and knowledge, "a selection . . . of the peculiar excellencies of every nation of the cosmos for the use of humanity" could and might be compiled.[103]

To accomplish this federal union, the only prerogatives that the nations had to forfeit were the right of the strong to oppress the weak, the right to kill and be killed, and the privilege of squandering money in armaments. As a result of the federal union, civilizations did not destroy the fruits of industry nor waste in battles the talents of the young; double-dealing diplomacy and the humiliation of one nation by another ceased; and the natural resources and energy once wasted in war were used for the advancement of the common interests and the good of the common estate. Moreover, all disputes among nations were settled by arbitration in a world court.[104]

Bellamy also delineated in *Looking Backward* the arrangements the International Council could make to permit travel and emigration through a debt and credit system. Any citizen could take his credit card to the local branch of the International Council that handled foreign travel; this agency would give the traveler the credit card of the nation to be visited; and the amount spent with the credit card during the visit to the country would be charged to the United States—in favor of the visited nation (*LB,* 116). Bellamy dreamed that many citizens of the ideal state would use their pecuniary equality, their vacations while they worked, and their leisure after retirement to visit and learn about other countries.[105]

Just as a section of the International Council handled travel, it also arranged for emigration and established a system of international indemnities. For example, if an American worker of twenty-one emigrated to France, the United States would lose the investment it had made in his rearing and education, and France would gain a citizen for whom it had to make an allowance to the United States. If, however, a worker who was nearing retirement emigrated to France, the United States would have to credit France with an allowance for his support. The only restriction to emigration applied to imbeciles: each nation was deemed fully responsible for such individuals; and, if they were permitted to emigrate, the nation from which they came had to guarantee their full maintenance (*LB,* 115).

Effects Upon Legislatures, Laws, and Crime

In answering both his adverse critics and his interested public, Bellamy expanded in *Equality* not only his criticism of the political-economic system of the nineteenth century but also his views of the role of the Congress, of laws, of crime, and of the wealth of the nation of the year 2000. In *Looking Backward* the Congress met every five years to assess the final report of the retiring president; and, if Congress proposed a law, that proposal would not be considered until its next meeting five years later (*LB,* 169). Although Bellamy had disposed of the state legislatures (*LB,* 168–69) and had given city governments more concern with the provision of leisure activities and the comfort of its citizens, he devoted more attention in *Equality* to government of and by the people and to showing what types of laws were needed, why crime was minimal, and what court system existed as a result of the ideal state.

As Bellamy explained in *Looking Backward,* the Congress was now so unimportant because the social order rested on fundamental principles which had settled once and for all the problems and the misunderstandings that had in turn created the mass of complex laws of the nineteenth century. To Bellamy, nearly all the laws of

that benighted period had dealt with property and trade problems;
in the year 2000 such legislation was unnecessary because individuals
owned only personal possessions, all citizens had an equal income,
and all commercial and industrial business was managed by the
federal government (*LB,* 169–70).

As Bellamy made clear in *Equality,* the whole system of criminal
justice of the nineteenth century was a mockery because the "intelligent man knew in his heart that the criminal and vicious were,
for the most part, what they were on account of neglect and injustice,
and an environment of depraving influences for which a defective
social order was responsible, and that, if righteousness were done,
society, instead of judging them, ought to stand with them in the
dock before a higher justice, and take upon itself the heavier con-
demnation" (*E,* 363). When the system had changed, many who
had been failures and criminals in the old society responded quickly
to the opportunity to be decent citizens; but there was a "large
residuum too hopelessly perverted, too congenitally deformed, to
have the power of leading a good life, however assisted" (*E,* 363).
For such criminals the new society had no toleration; it considered
them "morally insane" and segregated them in places of confinement
where they worked to produce their living and where they were not
permitted to produce their kind: "By this means the race, in the
first generation after the Revolution, was able to leave behind itself
forever a load of inherited depravity and base congenital instincts,
and so ever since it has gone on from generation to generation,
purging itself of its uncleanness" (*E,* 364).

Bellamy had presented in the *New Nation* some of the ideas advanced by labor organizations and the Populists concerning control
of government and its rescue from politicians and lawyers.[106] He
incorporated some of those same ideas in *Equality;* referendum,
initiative, and recall were the means of regulating Congress. Although the representatives of the people were chosen for a term,
that term was not irrevocable. In fact, the "vote of no delegate upon
any important measure can stand until his principals—or constit-
uents . . . —have had the opportunity to cancel it" (*E,* 274).
Because the telephone and telegraph made the public response easily
ascertained, the Congress had been "reduced to the exercise of the
functions of what you used to call congressional committees. The
people not only nominally but actually govern" (*E,* 274–75), for
they also have the right to propose to Congress the laws they desire.

If necessary, citizens could vote a hundred times a year upon laws that they themselves had introduced or upon any of the affairs of the nation that deeply concerned them, whether the problem was a new building or the world union. By making the legislature the reflector of the will of the citizenry, Bellamy answered his critics, such as B. O. Flower, who had feared that a dictatorship might develop in the ideal state.

Since an educated citizenry became the source of the laws of the nation, lawyers, whom Bellamy neither trusted nor respected, were no longer needed and became nonexistent. In the nineteenth century the complexity of the laws not only had made lawyers necessary but had also produced loopholes to permit the circumvention of justice. Such intricacies of the law and the desire of lawyers for money had made life secure for the rogues and the swindlers, by having trials postponed, by dragging out cases, by demanding retrials, or in the case of a murderer, by pleading insanity.[107] Although the lawyers of the nineteenth century had had to be intellectually brilliant, their famous legal library was now a museum; and the once-famous schools of law had also disappeared (*LB*, 168).

As Bellamy made very clear in *Looking Backward*, other branches of the federal government had also disappeared because many of the needs of the capitalistic system had become obsolete: it had no army, no navy, no military organization, no treasury department, no "excise or revenue services, no taxes or tax collectors" (*LB*, 169), no prisons, no juries, and no career judges. Many crimes had formerly been committed because of poverty or greed, but now economic equality and community spirit had alleviated those conditions and had so decreased crime that the complicated judicial system had been radically changed. In fact, the judiciary and police systems were the only existing examples of what the former government had had to provide for the protection of the citizens.

In *Looking Backward* Bellamy presented the outline of his new judicial system that he did not modify in *Equality*. The Supreme Court existed as the guardian of the Constitution; and, although he never specifically stated the nature of this document in the ideal state, he did state in *Equality* that the preamble of the American Declaration of Independence had contained the ideas and the guarantees of the ideal state (*E*, 16–17). Since law schools and lawyers no longer existed, the president selected and appointed the male minor judges, and the general-in-chief of the women's army appointed the females. Since the jury system had been disbanded, the judges were not only the jury but the prosecutor and the defense: three of them served when a citizen declared himself not guilty of the crime of which he was accused; two judges were appointed by the presiding judge to study and argue opposite sides of the case. After the presentation, the judge's decision was presented; and, if the other two judges did not agree with it, the case was retried (*LB*, 166). The same procedure was observed in the women's court; but, when a man and a woman were involved in a case, the two defending judges were a man and woman; and both had to confirm that the verdict was acceptable—just (*LB*, 211).

The changes that Bellamy made in the judiciary system were the result not only of his ideal state but of the criticism he had made of the judges, the courts, and the jury system in his writing before *Looking Backward* and after it in the *New Nation*. To restore respect for the law, Bellamy had advised that the administrators of justice be more honest and faithful in discharging their duties and that legal means be used, if necessary, to sharpen their consciences. In an article in the *Union* of 1872 Bellamy asserted that the inadequacy of the courts in rendering justice had caused the prevalence of lynchings. In the same newspaper and year he indicated that, since criminals and other transgressors of the law could vote for and elect their own judges, there could be no safeguard to insure an independent, honest judiciary; and he recommended that the judges be appointed but not for political reasons or party affiliations.[108]

In other articles in the *Springfield Union* Bellamy had also condemned the jury system as obsolete and inefficient and had suggested its reformation. In 1872 he had written rather satirically that the movement in New York to reform the court system was futile because it was impossible to find a juryman who was unacquainted with a case or who had thought nothing about it—unless he was a dolt or an idiot; for the newspapers not only informed all potential jurymen but also swayed their opinions.[109] In "An Absurdity of the Jury System" (1875) Bellamy stated that the jury system had become the enemy of the people because it could be swayed, as Professor Blakie of Scotland had indicated in his *Four Phases of Morals,* by popular passion. In this instance, Bellamy recommended that the jury system be replaced by some more efficient way of rendering justice; and he suggested that the decision of guilt or innocence could be determined by the judges. He recognized, however, that great caution would have to be exercised in the selection of judges if they were delegated such power.[110]

In 1892 and in 1893 articles in the *New Nation* Bellamy lambasted the court system of his time as one that defeated the administration of justice because of the delay created by the technicalities and the legal finesse of the system and because the high costs of the legal procedures made the attainment of justice too costly for the poor man to seek it. He defended the legal system of the ideal state by showing that justice would be quickly rendered, that all citizens could afford a hearing, that a case would not be purposefully muddled by the presence of lawyers, and that efficient and speedy execution of justice would have a sound moral effect upon the citizenry and would also stop lynchings.[111] In "Judicial Reform" (1877) in the *Union* Bellamy had aired some of the same ideas and criticisms he incorporated in his *New Nation* articles and in *Looking Backward;* but he had in turn found them in the report made by a commission that had been appointed to investigate the judicial system of the state of Massachusetts.[112]

Although Bellamy may have intended the judiciary system to be completed by the citizens of the ideal state, his proposed plan made no mention of how the inadequate judge could be dismissed; and, although he provided for a retrial of a case in which the judges did not reach a unanimous verdict, he also proposed no appeal to a higher court on the part of the accused. Although he made changes in *Equality* about the status of women, he did not mention that female judges would be as acceptable in any court case as the male ones would be.

Chapter Four

Intellectual, Religious, Domestic, and Other Innovations

Edward Bellamy rebelled at the enslavement of men to the monotonous treadmill of business, which destroyed morality and had stultifying effects upon the intellect. Little real life existed for the person reduced to a round of physical functions necessary to feed the body that lacked nourishment for the brain. The human happiness, security, and dignity that did exist, asserted Bellamy, were worthy of neither mankind nor God.[1] To him, the quest for the soul and the development of the mind were the prime purposes of life; and, if progress and inventions did not bring enlargement of the intellect, if they did not develop a more constant sense of sympathy with others, the steamship and the telegraph would merely be the playthings of men without souls. The world, Bellamy wrote, had been too long and too profitlessly concerned with the problem of "happy dying" because of the theologians. The stark conception of life that stressed mortification was narrow, and the renaissance could only truly begin when the benefit of asceticism had been replaced by that of development. And, wrote Bellamy, the one good result of Comte's Positivism was that more general attention was being given "to the more practical problems of happy living."[2]

Although Bellamy recognized man's desire for happiness as the positive impulse for his actions, he also thought that most acts regarded as virtuous contributed rather to the happiness and well-being of others: true progress depended upon the attainment of both individual and general felicity. But, to achieve this balance, both the individuality and the impersonality of mankind would have to be given their proper places in life. Although Bellamy, the realist, recognized that human beings had brutal passions and either selfish or ignorant ambitions, he also believed in their perfectibility—their being transfigured because of their attrition of the ideal—by developing their ability and desire to serve others in a cooperative society and by creating their interest in the Infinite.

As a result of such development, the passions of individuality which led to man's unhappiness would be used for the general achievement and the elevation of humanity.[3] To Bellamy, the virtuous, ideal man would be

> he whose spirit dwells among the stars and in all time, but whose hands are as deft with the most menial as with the mightiest tasks through which the soul of solidarity can find expression; who turns his hands with equal readiness to the founding of empires and to the washing of beggars' feet holding all tasks in equal honor, since with him the infinite motive overshadows the deed itself.[4]

To Bellamy, history, religion, and Herbert Spencer's theory of evolution promoted belief in mankind's achievement of perfection. In a speech written in the early 1870s Bellamy stated that no idea was historically more common to all ages of mankind than the belief that the world had before it an era of perfection—an era when human ignorance and social, political, and economic obstacles had been obliterated and when every human faculty became free for development and glorification.[5] In the manuscript "Liberty of the Press" Bellamy wrote that, if men believed that the tendency of human evolution was toward the higher and the better life, they had to sponsor whatever tended toward the "fullest expression of humanity" and that which induced its freest unfolding.[6] In "Religion" he asserted that God wished men to perfect themselves and become more like Him; and He intended this moral progress to result from love of Him and of fellowmen as well as from obedience to the moral law.[7]

In 1877 Bellamy wrote that Herbert Spencer, the predecessor of Darwin, had forecast a "completer perfection" for men and that he had shown man's "gradual development by the influence of his environment upon his faculties, the co-working of the external with the internal forces."[8] As Bellamy later explained in *Looking Backward,* human nature did not have to be radically altered to attain perfect ability or progress; for, as the conditions of life changed, the motives of human action would also change (*LB,* 45). Because the conditions of life had made men appear to be fundamentally base, proper changes in the environment would indicate for the first

time what "unperverted human nature really was like"—that its
essential qualities were "good, not bad . . . generous, not selfish,
pitiful, not cruel, sympathetic, not arrogant, godlike in aspirations,
instinct with divinest impulses of tenderness and self-sacrifice, im-
ages of God indeed" and "not the travesties upon Him they had
seemed" (LB, 234). When the adverse conditions of life that could
"have perverted angels" were removed, mankind, because of a "natural nobility" altered by adverse circumstances, had, "like a bent
tree, . . . sprung back to its normal uprightness" (LB, 234–35).

In his famous parable of the rosebush in Looking Backward Bellamy
made it clear that to be saved and perfected, mankind had to have
the proper, conducive environment (LB, 236). But he also argued
that one found even in an undesirable environment some individuals
who had reached a stage of development that would permit them
to live without coercive laws; and the presence of such people proved
that it was not necessary to change human nature before better
living conditions were inaugurated: it was only necessary that men
show a desire and a capability for new conditions before instituting
them.[9] Thus, Bellamy provided not only education but the Great
Revival to prepare citizens for an ethically healthy environment.

Religious Revival

As has been noted, Bellamy had had his own rebellion against
organized religion, but he had maintained the values and the standards of judgment instilled in him by his parents. Like his ancestor
the famous Reverend Joseph Bellamy, Edward sought to restore
what he himself considered the true religion; but, unlike his ancestor, he did not have a conventional attitude toward God, nor did
he believe that any one religious sect had found the true interpretation. In fact, Bellamy regarded the multiplicity of religious creeds
as responsible for both mental confusion and social conflict. When
he formed his "Religion of Solidarity," and, later in Looking Backward and Equality, the religion of the ideal state, he, like Matthew
Arnold, dispensed with theology and sects but maintained the spirit
and morality of Christianity which he seemingly combined with the
enthusiasm for humanity of Auguste Comte and others.[10] In his
philosophy of solidarity and also in his articles in the Springfield
Union Bellamy denounced selfishness and practices that contributed
neither to individual nor to general welfare;[11] and he strongly ad-

vocated that unselfishness in loving and in serving others was conducive to individual and general happiness, peace, and morality.[12]
Since the highest religion sponsored love, trust, and service, Bellamy
expressed the hope that the day would arrive when men who lived
honest, moral, unselfish lives would not be considered heretics if
they did not subscribe to some religious sect; for, in such a future
era, the man whose life was right would not, could not, be considered
to be wrong in his beliefs.[13]

In editorials in the *Springfield Union* Bellamy revealed to the
student of his life and development his preparation for the religion
he was to present in *Looking Backward* and in *Equality*. In "Christianity as a National Law" and in "Christianity and Civilization"
he evinced his firm belief in the need of religion not only by individuals but by society. Individually, religion explained to man
his relationship with the finite and the Infinite; it formed his ideas,
his character, and his spiritual life; it regulated his physical life;
and it helped him not only to live but to die. Religion was, therefore,
comparable to the soil that nourished the tree;[14] and, if mankind
were to be aided by the social order, all laws, all actions, all intellectual and cultural activities had to be based upon moral and religious concepts (which were but two faces of the same medal).[15]

In these same editorials Bellamy also made it clear that the ag-
gregate morality of a nation depended upon the daily religious
practices of the citizens who comprised it. Any reform in the social
state had to be accomplished not only by scientific discoveries of
the natural truths or laws but also by the study of moral truths and
by their practice—and the practice would be the result of the education of the mind and heart of man.[16] In his book reviews of the
later 1870s Bellamy cited the views of writers who confirmed his
own concepts. In his review of George MacDonald's *St. George and
St. Michael,* a novel about the Civil War in England that portrayed
how fiercely people could fight because of their different ideologies,
Bellamy wrote: "The deeper moral of the tale is the conclusion to
which the hero comes at last, that it is vain to battle for political
liberty and a very little thing to have gained, unless the soul is free
from the bondage of selfishness and sin."[17] To Bellamy, "The world
is set right by love, and this demands confidence in goodness and
trust in God. Positive forces are the saviors of humanity—clear,
strong, mighty beliefs in the good time coming, and in the power

of Christian truth and grace to bring it about. The doubters and devilers cannot march in the van of this army."[18]

Bellamy delivered jeremiads and waged war against the "moral depression" of his era. He cited the indictment by Mrs. Oliphant in her novel *At His Gate* of the smug and pious Philistines as the true criminals of society who acted according to the principle of business that anyone had the right to get the better of another if he could.[19] The trinity of Wall Street, wrote Bellamy, was the world, the flesh, and the devil;[20] and in many other reviews and editorials he denounced the lustful worship of material things that led to corrupt and piratical business practice, veniality in the legislatures, sensual enjoyments, and distrust of others. Although the nation was Christian in name, its mode of life was comparable to Greek paganism; for such epicurean luxuriousness, or the desire to attain it, was sapping the foundations of true manliness, undermining physical stamina, and destroying the ability or the desire to cultivate and to exercise moral standards.[22]

As for the different churches, they had more concern about their particular religious concepts than they had for basically religious practices. Besides their selfish sectarian interests, they were dissipating their energies in destructive religious squabbles and were even denouncing as unorthodox such practicing Christians as Dwight Lyman Moody[23] and Professor David Swing.[24] Like the materialists who were their members, the churches were emphasizing the need for exclusive and finer churches; and, in building them, they made shrewd real estate investments when they selected the sites.[25] As for the ministers, they had no leadership: they were submissive to the rule of the rich who supported the churches and could hire and fire them. Since the ministers could no longer be independent enough to tell the people the truth—that their morality was divorced from important religious dictates—Bellamy advocated that the ministers should be independent in order to fulfill their real duties.[26]

As for the real duties of the ministers and their churches, Bellamy had no doubt: their work was to combat the evils of the era, to improve society through the inculcation of positive faith in the capabilities of universal truth and genuine goodness to produce improvement, and to instruct people in and to encourage their practice of virtue and godliness. The true role of the church was to follow the example of Christ by going about doing good and by carrying the principles of good living into the slums; and it needed, instead of periodic revivals, to be persevering and stable in its work.[27] As for the ministers themselves, they had to be capable of working with people, of using their responsibilities for the common benefit, of maintaining close contact with public affairs, of being brave enough to do what they thought was right, and of spending more time in their studies in order to create sermons that would hold the interest of even the most intelligent members of their congregations.[28]

Bellamy also noted with interest that the religious agitation of his period was distinguished by the fact that rapid changes were occurring in the doctrines of the churches and that the most pronounced characteristics of these changes were toward more philosophical and liberal attitudes regarding Christianity. Bellamy, who advocated that men forget ritualism—which could become rutism—and creeds which were divisive and absorbing—hoped that the tendencies and changes of his time would lead to a perfected Christianity.[29] To aid in such a development, he recommended that those training for the ministry no longer attend seminaries but be so broadly educated that they would have not only a broad knowledge of human nature but also common sense. The theologians, who were noted for their whole-souled intellectual combativeness, were waging pitched battles among themselves instead of uniting to fight the social and moral evils that delayed the perfection of men and their society.[30]

Bellamy's advocacy of such changes in the church and in ministers was based not only upon his views relative to solidarity but also upon many of the advanced books that he read about religion in the 1870s. Bellamy regarded favorably Dr. J.G. Holland's desire to have a religion without creeds; E. Maitland's *By and By, An Historical Romance of the Future* (1873), which portrayed a church in which the ecclesiastical and dogmatic organizations have died but in which the general culture has absorbed the message of Christ; the Reverend Minot J. Savage's *Christianity and the Science of True Manhood* (1873), which advocated casting off the "merely traditional and nonessential" and preserving the essentials of religion—those of divine revelation; and Dr. James F. Clarke's *Common Sense in Religion* (1874), which proposed that men use their "common sense quite uncommon" and their judgment rather than rigid textual interpretations of the Bible.[31]

In regard to more intelligent interpretations of the Bible, Bellamy expressed in his reviews his appreciation of the scholarly studies that were investigating the myths and legends of the past and that, because of their bearing upon those of the Bible, were creating broader interpretations. Among the many men he mentioned as such investigators, he cited Max Muller, whose books he placed on the reading list he concocted for his son Paul. In an editorial Bellamy reported upon a lecture given by English poet Gerald Massey that portrayed the influence of the Zoroastrians of Persia upon the Hebrew conception of the devil, the changing views of the devil in different countries and epochs, and the modern tendency to regard him as a personification of the evil that dwelt in the heart of men.[32]

Bellamy also noted in 1873 and 1876 in "Literary Notices," that Samuel Lee in *The Bible Regained* and George Merriam in *A Living Faith* had denied the existence of eternal punishment; that the Reverend John Miller in *Fetich or Doctrinalism* had delivered a polemic against the Reverend Dr. Charles Dodge, the chief exponent of Calvinism, and had maintained that God had to be regarded as having the most essential quality of love for others and that true worship of God excited love for one's fellows. To be a Christian was to have born within one's soul a new affection for Christ, for God, and for everything good which would be not a mere sentiment but a reigning, motivating love.[33] Others whose books also advocated a practical application of Christian ethics in daily living as a means of improving humanity and society and whose works were reviewed by Bellamy included Dr. Cyrus A. Bartol (*The Rising Faith,* 1874); and Matthew Arnold (*God and the Bible,* 1875; *Last Essays on Church and Religion,* 1877).[34]

Bellamy also followed with interest the effect of Darwin's theory of evolution upon the churches, and he wrote in 1875 in the *Union* that the aim of the true student must be to make the unity of science and religion manifest, for both were branches of science—if the elements of religion were grasped correctly and if science recognized true wisdom and was inspired by the right motives. To Bellamy, "the great necessity of modern thought" was that science and religion, standing on the same footing, resolve their conflicts by finding their way through "whatever jungles of physical or theological error" had led to confusion. In a review of 1876 Bellamy reported that Professor Asa Gray in *Darwiniana* (1876) had discovered that the theory of evolution did not conflict with Christianity and that the evolutionary theory had given Christianity a more sublime truth.[35]

Bellamy wrote with knowledge of a great many minor American religious sects, such as the Millerites, and regarded Swedenborgianism and Higher Pantheism as subtle and fascinating religious philosophies; but he was most interested in the Evangelical Alliance, which earned his respect for quite obvious reasons: this movement proposed the unity of all Christian sects for influence and for practical work, and its motto was "Variety and Unity." To Bellamy, this slogan expressed the social ideal, "the secret of the universal frame of things," and the perfect base for the universal church. The principle of variety would permit intellectual liberty relative to metaphysical interpretation and would end, therefore, the theological efforts to enforce uniformity of belief in matters of dogma. Enforced uniformity of interpretation and belief was not only dangerous because it precluded growth but also impossible to attain in a large body of people; and, moreover, such enforcement was not essential to real unity of belief about fundamental principles.[36] Unity of belief was essential, however, about the purposes and main elements; and it was necessary for combined, associated, effective results. Institutions existed to accomplish certain types of work; the principles and laws which were their bases and which gave them their power were only the means to achieve the desired end. The church, therefore, did not exist to save its doctrines; but, through teaching the basic principles of religion, it existed to save the world around it—humanity and society—and thus achieve the only unity necessary.[37]

Although Bellamy portrayed in *Looking Backward* the unified social order as resting upon the principle of the brotherhood of man, he said very little about the actual conditions of the churches except that no national church and no official clergymen existed (*LB*, 229, 221). If a professional minister existed, he was supported financially by his parishioners who paid the state the income he received and also paid the government for the public hall in which the minister preached (*LB*, 222–23). Most citizens preferred, however, to listen to sermons delivered into their homes by radio—a sermon they chose to hear because it was prepared by a very intelligent citizen. In *Looking Backward* Julian West listens with his host to the sermon delivered by Dr. Barton in which are presented the essential tenets of the brotherhood of man (*LB*, 231, 229, 225–26).

Bellamy's critics—among them Anna Dawes, William Higgs, Michael Maher, A.G. Sedgwick, and General F. Walker[38]—indicated that his social order was opposed to accepted Christian beliefs, that it was only through conflict with evil that men developed their souls, that the worldly life was unimportant since men were to seek to attain the afterlife, that Christ had announced that the poor would exist forever, that God had ordained that man would forever have to earn his bread with the sweat of his brow, and that material things were unnecessary for the development of the soul. In fact, one newspaper review stated that not a word about Christianity appeared in *Looking Backward* and that the millenium that had arrived in it was not Christian since religion had had very little to do with bringing about the results portrayed.[39]

In his "Talks on Nationalism," in his letters, and in "Looking Forward" Bellamy carefully defined the religion that was the basis of Nationalism and showed that its aims and principles were Christian. The basic principle was the brotherhood of man, and the acceptance of this basic principle obliged men to assume their responsibilities for one another and to recognize the fraternal cooperation was not only a scientific method of producing wealth but the only moral basis of society.[40] Nationalism followed the mandates of Christ because it taught man to love his neighbor as himself, established love as the basis of society, made it the duty of the strong to help the weak, and preached unselfishness—the root and flower of all true religion.[41]

The establishment of the social order based on the Golden Rule of Christ would result in His second coming; but His coming would be in the hearts of men; it would lead to the application of His principles to every phase of life; and Christ, instead of being defied, would be truly deified.[42] The social order would no longer be a mockery of the Founder of Christianity, and the absence of poverty in it would not be in conflict with His teachings—which were, in this instance, to be interpreted in a relative sense. To those who questioned whether economic reforms were necessary for the achievement of morality, Bellamy replied that moral reformation would not solve a problem that was basically economic; for, if the moral stigmas of the system were removed, the economic defects would still remain. Furthermore, Christ would not sanction the economic conditions that caused strife, for His had been a message of goodwill, and He had hoped that men would develop the moral qualities that would lead to their perfection.[43] Bellamy assured his public that the future of religion was promising since every religious denomination contained a radical group that desired not only a broader religion but a practiced Christianity.[44]

In *Equality* not only Dr. Barton but Dr. Leete, Edith's father, explains to West the inadequacy of the church, the ministers, and teachers during the Great Revival and the Revolution. Although these characters repeat the charges made against such professionals in *Looking Backward,* they now attack their sins of omission, their subservience to plutocracy, and their callous ability to ignore the misery of the people in the nineteenth century—a situation described as comparable to the Black Hole of Calcutta. Moreover, Bellamy verifies these views of nineteenth-century degradation and exploitation of the working man by introducing not only a history of the period by Storiot, but also his own satiric "Parable of the Water Tank."

Bellamy presents in this famous parable of the Capitalist and his market the plight of the laborer in the nineteenth century: the worker, who is paid one cent for every bucket of water he brings to the tank (the Market), is charged two cents for every bucket he purchases. This profit soon exhausts the pennies of the working class; the tank is filled to overflowing; economic crisis develops; people suffer from thirst; owners of the tank, who refuse to give them water, seek soothsayers to provide the thirsty citizens with explanations; the owners finally use the water for their pleasure after they have hired guards from among the thirsty to protect the tank and use the water; and the crisis occurs again when the tank is refilled. The agitators who try to teach the people about the truth of their situation are finally believed by the citizens, they assume full responsibility for the tank, and "there was no more any thirst in the land . . . [and the people] do dwell together in unity" (*E,* 203).

As has been stated elsewhere, the basic principle of the Revolution that created the ideal society was Christ's Golden Rule "of equal and the best treatment for all." However, two sets of causes for the Revolution are very carefully explained to Julian in *Equality:* "First, the general, necessary, and fundamental cause" and "second, the proximate or provoking causes which, within certain limits, determined when it actually did take place, together with the incidental features" (*E,* 305). The important fundamental cause was the growth of intelligence and knowledge among the people because of the availability of printed material in the nineteenth century; this awakening led to the realization that political equality had to be accompanied by economic equality: "the equalization of the distribution of work and wealth (*E,* 307)."

Storiot in his history of the Revolution describes the reform movements of the pre-Civil War period as being halted by the Civil War and identifies the war itself as having given power and great wealth to the capitalists. Dr. Leete, however, omits this period: he claims that the era of the 1870s provided the second, provocative cause of the Revolution—the economic distress of the citizens had continued until they had sought and found their solution in the Revolution and the creation of the ideal state (*E,* 308). To assure Julian that statistics prove the power and wealth of the plutocrats, Dr. Leete obtains from his library a book of statistics relative to 1893 prepared by the census office. In that year it was "estimated that out of sixty-two billions of wealth in the country a group of millionaires and multimillionaires, representing three one-hundreths of one per cent of the population, owned twelve billions, or one fifth [of the wealth]. Thirty-three billions of the rest was owned by a little less than nine percent of the American people . . . (*E,* 321). The estimates of 1889 and 1891 indicated that the nation had now become divided into classes—"the rich, the middle, and the working class"—and that the rich, the "one and four tenths percent of the population," possessed "seventy percent of the total wealth" (*E,* 321–22). Although America had been the only place in the world until after the Civil War in which a degree of economic equality never before known had existed, the plutocrats had within thirty years made tremendous strides toward complete expropriation of the wealth of the nation (*E,* 322).

The new social order that corrected such inequities of wealth by endorsing economic equality was attributed by Bellamy to the effect of the great enthusiasm for humanity which, with its deep feeling of the brotherhood of mankind, had brought people together; and, though this humane movement had not been consciously Godward in its early aspirations, it had resulted in the true finding of God and in a true understanding of the words of Christ. When men had experienced love and unselfishness and when they had welcomed all men as their brothers, they had only then learned the true significance of "God the Father" and of the words which expressed in *Equality* the religion of love that was the basis of the ideal society:

" 'If we love one another God dwelleth in us and his love is perfected in me.' 'He that loveth his brother dwelleth in the light.' 'If any man say I love God, and hateth his brother, he is a liar.' 'He that loveth not his brother, abideth in death.' 'God is love and he that dwelleth in love dwelleth in me.' 'Every one that loveth knoweth God.' 'He that loveth not knoweth not God.' " (*E,* 268–69)

Although these statements unified the nation, release from the authoritarian ecclesiastical system which had resulted in a variety of thought made men's engrossing pursuit in the year 2000 the search "after knowledge concerning the nature and destiny of man and his relation to the spiritual and material infinity of which he is a part" (*E,* 264–67; 284). Since no organization has solved the problem or presented the solution, each man is obliged to discover his own religion or interpretation; and society as a whole—because it, like that of "The Blindman's World," does not rely upon the authority of the past—anticipates having greater knowledge of the soul and of God and believes that there is no limit to what might be known about man's destiny. The changes made in the ecclesiastical system are to contribute, therefore, to progress in the science of the soul and to the knowledge of its relationship to the Eternal and the Infinite; and this achievement, in turn, is to contribute to an increase in human happiness (*E,* 264–68). The most important aspect of the ideal state is not that it will supply men with material comforts but that it will free them from bondage to the world of the flesh and the devil and will then lead them to the normal life of the true Kingdom of God in which neither humanity nor Christ will any longer be crucified (*E,* 385).

In *Looking Backward* and in *Equality* Bellamy gave to every man in his ideal state his own engrossing problem: the solution of the relationship of man to the finite and the Infinite; and he assured for every youth a life free from the painful, disillusioning recognition that his noble dreams or interpretations of the Bible were not in accord with the practices of his world. As a result of his own religious experience, his philosophy, and his broad knowledge of the religious movements of his own day, Bellamy formed a belief free of dogmas, rituals, creeds, and superstitions—which were socially divisive and

intellectually stupifying—and created a religion that was emotionally and practically unifying in its stress upon the love and duty of
man to God and to his fellowmen. In this religion and its practice
Bellamy not only fulfilled the dream of many Americans—as has
been indicated by Page Smith in his recently published *The Rise of
Industrial America* (1984)—but one that forced Americans to develop
the impersonal, unifying characteristics of the "Religion of Solidarity." To Bellamy, as to Plato and Charles Kingsley, religion
meant very little if it did not preach liberty, equality, and fraternity,
and if it did not lead to the moral world so many men had dreamed
of man's achieving. "Think you," wrote Bellamy in his journal,
"there is any thought dearer to the mind of God than that his
children should be brothers?"[45]

Physical and Mental Education

Bellamy has Julian West state in *Looking Backward* that he has
taken but a "slight interest in educational matters in his former
life" (*LB*, 181). This statement does not reflect the views of his
creator, who had shown an intense interest in education in his articles
in the *Springfield Union*, the *Golden Age*, and the *Daily News*, and
who had stated in his first lyceum address not only that education
was a topic that had "long occupied . . . earnest thought" but also
that the educational reform movement was the most important one
of his era.[46] In his lyceum address Bellamy evinced thoughts about
education that could be used to introduce what he recommended
in his utopian novels, for he stated that the success or failure of the
democratic state depended upon the ability of the people to make
intelligent decisions and to avoid being corrupted. Individually, the
happiness of man, his human dignity, his ability and his desire to
perfect not only himself but his social order, as well as his lack of
religious superstition, depended upon his being educated.[47]

In articles prior to the publication of *Looking Backward* Bellamy
was critical of the inequalities of education because he regarded
them as endangering the unity, prosperity, and political future of
the nation.[48] Because of the employment of young boys on farms
and in mills, factories and shops, and also because of the thousands
of immigrants imported as cheap labor, Bellamy warned that too
many citizens were illiterate for the safety of democracy.[49] He maintained that the lack of a proper education also resulted not only in

unskilled workmen who had difficulty in finding work but also in crime and in loafing.[50] Moreover, he observed somewhat amusingly that the disparities in the education of men and women that existed led to better education for the women, since fewer of them went to work during the school-age period, and this difference resulted not only in limited mutual social enjoyment of men and women but also contributed to the increasing number of New England old maids![51]

To remedy the lack of education, Bellamy advocated not only compulsory education but also night schools for employed youths and immigrants, and he urged that adults use the libraries and debating societies to increase their knowledge, their happiness, and their usefulness.[52] He also suggested reforms in administration and curriculum that would more effectively fulfill the purpose of education: to develop in students intelligence, right principles, and "patriotic goodness."[53] To accomplish these objectives, he advocated that teachers awaken the dormant faculties of students, discover and develop their innate abilities, and teach them to think with independence.[54] Bellamy urged that good, well-trained teachers be employed, that they no longer teach by rote, and that their originality of method be unhampered.[55]

Because Bellamy valued stimulating, original teachers, he disagreed with John Quincy Adams and Charles T. Adams, Jr., who advocated the hiring of more superintendents of schools who had been trained in the science of education. Bellamy feared that such administrators would make the educational system a machine that would suppress originality in teaching.[56] He staunchly advocated that a board of professional educators have the responsibility not only of selecting teachers but also of choosing texts and of determining general policies of school management and methods.[57] But he also had his own ideas about the literature that children should read, since its influence was second to that of the home. The best literature for those aged seven to fourteen, he felt, was the early national literature of their country, the fairy tales of Germany, *The Arabian Nights,* the Bible, and the works of Homer—works both to please and to stir the imagination. After fourteen, children were to read biographies and travel books that would teach them about real life. Although Bellamy did not recommend didactic Sunday School literature, he admitted that mushy stories filled with lifeless morality could do little harm.[58]

Since Bellamy felt that education improved the physical being and the mind, he encouraged the enlargement of the curriculum to include instruction in the physiology of sex, the laws of health, political science, the different occupations and trades, and calesthenics.[59] He advocated that the schools develop the physical and social abilities of students during their formative years.[60] Moreover, he specifically recommended athletics as of great value for young men, because exercise kept them from vice and prevented depraved, feeble bodies inclined to unhealthful and excessive appetites and desires. In his journals Bellamy had noted the influence of illness upon his own reactions and upon his sensitivity to nature, and he had written in the *Springfield Union* that it was no strange doctrine to the people of his day that "the influence of the body on the soul is as great as the influence of the soul upon the body."[61]

In his editorials in the *Union,* he had declared that the United States was a "nervous, dyspeptic, and bilious nation" and that the era of 1870 was one of nerves.[62] He warned his readers who, instead of walking, rode in buggies: their legs "were withering into spindleshanks through lack of use" and they were being taken to their graves by torpid livers and dyspepsia. Also contributing to physical and mental decline were the indoor life of factory and shop that had replaced the outdoor agricultural existence; the prevalence of earning a living by the wits rather than by manual labor; the strife and competition of the business world; rivalry, ostentation, and ambition in the social life which kept noses to the grindstone; bad food, poor sanitation, and poor ventilation; the too-tight lacing of women's garments; and the inability of people to enjoy their leisure.[63] To correct such degenerating conditions, Bellamy advised *Union* readers to give more attention to the art of living; for people should not die in the prime of life but should "die in old age . . . like the dropping of a ripe apple to the ground, unaccompanied by wrench or strain of any sort."[64] To the "coming race," wrote Bellamy, the laws of health would be a part of religion, with the motto of "Healthy minds in healthy bodies." In this future period material and immaterial things would receive attention, and the body would no longer be ignored or contemned, for it would then be given the respect once awarded it by the Greeks.[65]

Bellamy included many of these concepts in *Looking Backward* and *Equality*. Because of the emphasis upon physical culture and the laws of hygiene in the year 2000, the educational system of the ideal state has as its objective the mental, physical, and moral progress of mankind (*E,* 145, 147–52, 283–84; *LB,* 238). When Bellamy portrayed in *Looking Backward* a physically and mentally healthy populace, he attributed its fitnesses to economic equality, to education, and to better living conditions. Men no longer work long hours at a job they dislike in an unsanitary factory: their work is inspiring; the factory conditions are healthy; and the hours are regulated by the arduousness, the danger, and the distastefulness of the task (*LB,* 210, 277, 182).

Among the other changes improving working conditions are the eradication not only of the mental strain induced by anxiety over the uncertainty of being able to earn a living for one's family, but also of the ceaseless battle for life and economic security engendered by the old competitive world. With these nineteenth-century characteristics gone, suicide and insanity are less prevalent; the luxurious debauchery of the mind and the body by the wealthy and the soul-and-mind-killing life of the workman which had made him a walking dead man have been removed; and the half-clad, brutalized working children of the poor have been replaced by the carefully nurtured children of the year 2000, whose heritage is better than that of their forebears because of the principle of sexual selection in mating (*LB,* 266, 182, 265, 219). Because of the improved conditions provided by the ideal state, the fetid air and the death-dealing water of the old tenement district have disappeared. Moreover, the bad foods of the nineteenth century have been replaced by the pure, unadulterated ones of the ideal society, which also supplies the public with carefully prepared meals from communal kitchens (*LB,* 265, 182, 227).

In articles in the *Nationalist* and the *New Nation* Bellamy continued to express his concern about the education of poor children. He suggested not only that compulsory education be enforced but that impoverished parents who needed the income of their working children be aided by the state. He argued that to reform society or to bring about a new world required preparing the future citizen during his period of greatest plasticity. Moreover, if required education removed the children from the factories, the result would be more employment of adults.[66]

In the *New Nation* Bellamy reversed his early attitude about vocational education as a means of decreasing unemployment; he now thought that having more trained workers would lead only to an increase in production, which in turn would create gluts on the market and, thus, unemployment. If a young person were fortunate enough to discover the vocation for which he was best suited, he might also find the door shut to training for his occupation because of the protective policy of the labor unions which limited the number of apprentices.[67] Bellamy also warned that the outlook for those educated for the professions could be bleak because a superfluity of professional people could lead to decreased incomes. Professional education would also be a handicap to those who had to resort to manual labor. However, this situation would not exist in the ideal state: trained individuals would be wanted, and all qualified, interested individuals would have the opportunity to develop their abilities and to employ them for the benefit of society.[68]

In his remarks in *Equality* about mental and physical education in the ideal state Bellamy stressed that schools and teachers would be liberated from the influence of pressure groups, for they would have the freedom of thought and the originality permitted in the nineteenth century only to those who taught the dead languages (*E*, 335–36, 401). Moreover, mediocrity in teaching would also pass away, since the use of radio (telephone) and television (electroscope) would make it possible for students of the decentralized and community universities to hear the lectures of the greatest teachers of their day (*E*, 246–47).

Bellamy also emphasized adult education, for he thought that education really began only after the age of twenty-one when the citizens were more ardent, interested, and effective learners (*E*, 249–50). After the ideal state had been attained, the adults and the children who had been deprived of education flocked into the schools (*E*, 361–63). As Julian West discovered, great stress was placed on physical education, and the student took pride throughout his life in his physical fitness. All students were taught physiology, the laws of hygiene, and the science of medicine (*E*, 144; 283–84). The greatest result of this program was seen in the physical condition of women, who had benefited from the free, unfettered life they led and from the educational opportunities provided for them (*E*, 147–49; 256).

Because of the physical and mental education provided the citizens of the year 2000, every phase of individual and national life was affected, for such education had been the boon that had made the ideal state possible (*E*, 248). The relationship of the successful education of the citizenry and of the ideal state was a reciprocal one, for the success of the government depended upon the procurement of enlightened, wise, thoughtful, and analytical citizens (*E,* 247–48; 256); upon educated, effficient, and productive workers (*E,* 378); upon the best-prepared leaders and administrators (*E,* 256); and upon a unified and homogenous citizenry. Such an education would decrease superstition and ignorance, lead to the disappearance of divisive religious sectarianism, and create a replacement—the unifying principle of brotherly love (*E,* 259). Moreover, a more refined and cultured society would place less emphasis upon gross individuality, and more intellectual and aesthetic interests would result in less play of the brutal animal instincts (*LB,* 164, 177, 179–81; *E,* 412).

Because of the education that Bellamy sponsored and because of the improved living conditions that he advocated, he was able to forecast in *Looking Backward* that the citizens of the year 2000 would live to be eighty or ninety years of age and that men at the retirement age of forty-five, when the most enjoyable years of life would begin, would be physically and mentally younger than those of thirty-five had been in the nineteenth century (*LB,* 160). Although Bellamy was correct about the effect of an improved environment upon longevity, he did not foresee the personal and the socioeconomic problems of the aged that are today receiving so much attention and study by gerontologists and economists. Bellamy was farsighted, however, when he delegated so much voting power to the retired, older citizens; even today the majority of voters belong to this group, which expresses more interest in governmental affairs at the polls than do the younger citizens.

Because of the educational system he proposed, Bellamy welcomed the use of all inventions that had been approved by the government agencies, for he planned that displaced workers would merely be shifted to other positions or be retrained for work for which they had not been educated. The displaced worker of the trades in Bellamy's society was not trained just for a specific, lifelong occupation; he was prepared for the industrial world in which a citizen could expect two or three different jobs or positions during his stint as a laborer. Bellamy planned a broad general education from the first grade through college for all citizens of his state in order to prepare them not only for their three-year term devoted to doing the "dirty work" of the nation but for the discovery of their innate abilities and capabilities. Individuals who did not desire or warrant such additional educational investments were not permitted to sit at home and enjoy their economic equality, but were assigned until their retirement to do the "dirty work" of the nation; and, like the American citizens who served in the WPA (Works Progress Administration, 1935–43), these laborers could redecorate the schools, collect the debris that clutters the country, plant forests, and perform other needed work for the benefit of the population and future generations.

Liberated Women

Bellamy's attitude toward women in general in the early period of his writing was neatly summarized in his statement: "Woman is divine, women are human."[69] Bellamy, who recognized that Christianity had been perfecting for over a thousand years the idealization of woman,[70] regarded her as divine because, in giving birth to a child, she created a soul. Since she was seen as bearing the burden of humanity, men worshipped her because of an instinct of race and not of sex.[71] As for the "human women," Bellamy regarded them as being the natural enemies of religious and social progress: because of their ignorance, their superstitions, and their inferior status, they were conservative clingers to the status quo, to the church, and to any social institutions that protected them. Women, "the priestesses of sham,"[72] embodied the social tyranny of convention not only in their conservative support of tradition but in their lives, stunted and warped by societal traditions.

Bellamy observed in his early published and unpublished fiction that social conventions forced females to adopt two or three attitudes when in society and to act unnaturally about church festivals, parties, and dressing; however, when they were alone, they were candid, comradely, and unaffected.[73] Because of their social and economic status, women were forced to hunt for husbands to maintain them; but the giggling, flirting, gossiping, bargaining, and conversationally affected women were very difficult to sustain or to adore.[74] But Bellamy understood the factors that produced such women. In an unpublished short story, he delineated the maturation of Ethel Damon, who when younger had been free to romp and play with her brother Tom. As she matured, Ethel became increasingly aware of and indignant about the injustice of the distinctions made between the sexes: she recognized that the social conventions—"a grand repressive scheme" of restrictions—separated her from life and turned her into a straight and narrow path which imprisoned her, humiliated her, and retarded the development of her mind. As her brother observed her change, he was glad he was not a woman because of the "hemmed in, cramped, and precise existence they led." Bellamy's conclusion: "If God had depended for volunteers there would have been no women. But He conscripted souls . . . for duty."[75]

In his editorials in the *Union* Bellamy suggested that the conventions that made it impossible for women to move in society without an escort hampered the enterprising woman, and he urged that the safe reality of the situation be presented or that a bureau of escorts be established. In fact, he wrote, the public sentiment relative to the protection of females seemed to spring from the feeling that women were weak in mind and incompetent in taking care of themselves, and that fathers, husbands, and brothers had proprietary rights over their female relatives or their mates. Women needed to assert their right to be regarded as independent, self-controlled members of the community: such a position would free their fathers and brothers from the necessity of shooting their daughter's or sister's seducer![76]

When in 1873 the Women's Congress convened in New York City, Bellamy recognized the importance of the meeting. It indicated to him that the suffrage movement was ceasing to be a purely political question and was merging into the broader, deeper question of women's general status in society. Women gravely discussed at this convention questions of social improvement, such as dress, coeducation of the sexes, the moral and the physical aspects of motherhood, and the rearing of children. If suffrage were extended to women, wrote Bellamy, it would indicate the readiness of the public "for a great and profound revolution in the status of the sex."[77]

Although some females and their organizations, like the Illinois Association Opposed to the Extension of Suffrage to Women, published literature that suggested that women remain in the home, others found that the industrial revolution provided jobs for them, and from 1870 to 1890 the number of women over sixteen employed in factories, offices, and stores grew from 384,819 to 1,707,415. Moreover, women had pioneered in the medical profession; by 1880, nearly two hundred women had become ministers; seventy-five of them were lawyers; and Bellamy had remarked in 1873 that an "eruption of women" had occurred in journalism.[78] Because he believed that work was an honor to women as well as to men and that it might also be the women's way to "life, liberty, and happiness,"[79] he advised the mothers who read the *Union* in 1873 to give their daughters Phebe C. Hanaford's *Women of the Century* as a means of stimulating them to emulate the women farmers, printers, brokers, editors, lecturers, and lawyers depicted there.[80] In the same year Bellamy twitted the male students who had forced the dismissal of women students from colleges by stating that they feared the women would raise the academic standards, and he declaimed such male actions as contemptible.[81] As for the medical profession that would crush a women who entered it, Bellamy informed its male members that they belonged to the Dark Ages and not to the nineteenth century.[82]

In 1877 Bellamy called attention in "The New Magazines" to a publication in the *Radical Review* in which Henry Edger proposed that the state support women[83]—a plan that doubtless appealed to Bellamy both because of his desire to enfranchise women and because of his wish to emancipate men, who, when they married, would not be free to study nature, books, and their relationship to the finite and the Infinite. However, Bellamy, the father and author of *Looking Backward,* stated in an interview with Frances Willard that he did not want his son Paul to get ahead of his sister Marion in "opportunity so far as I can influence the forms of society. I would make women absolutely independent of men to the extent the material values are concerned,—thus sweeping away at one stroke the great temptation the physically weaker had to go wrong and the most potent weapon of the physically stronger in putting her at disadvantage and himself to shame."[84]

Given the ideas that Bellamy so freely expressed in his articles, literary reviews, and interviews, the Edith Leete of *Looking Backward* is not surprising in being portrayed as an educated, serene, frank, womanly but employed woman who also enjoyed economic equality. Although Bellamy created a sphere for the activities of women which he said provided for their individuality, he did not seek, like other reformers of his period, to obliterate popular concepts about their innate differences. He did present the new order as "a paradise for women" because their own industrial army enabled them to lead full, developed lives and to have "no unnatural rivalry" with men

(*LB,* 209–12). In the year 2000 women were also freed from marital sexual slavery, were no longer martyrs to household chores, received equal educational opportunities, were economically independent, were free to enjoy outdoor life and to be themselves when in the company of men, and were respected and honored for bearing and nursing children.[85]

Before the publication of *Equality* Bellamy stressed in his articles that Nationalism was the only plan that would insure freedom, dignity, economic independence, and equality of opportunity for women because their status was so involved with other social questions. Moreover, he felt Nationalism was the only socialism that would be efficacious for women because it alone secured them economic equality: the European socialists, who advocated equal pay for equal work, would not equally aid women who bore children and were unable to work or those whose physical natures disqualified them as equal competitors of men. Bellamy frequently stated that economic equality would end prostitution and the sexual servility in marriage of women. Even if the English Methodist Church eliminated "obey" from the marriage ceremony, only Nationalism would truly end the necessity of a women's obedience to her master.[86] Nationalism was, in fact, the "Declaration of Independence" of women.[87]

In *Equality* Bellamy repeated his portrayal of the healthy, happy women of *Looking Backward.* But because of the criticism he had received from some suffragettes, he now also pictured them as the equals of men and incorporated some of the themes he had harped upon in journals, editorials, and reviews. Because of their education, their independent economic status, and their newly acquired self-confidence, women no longer clung to and supported inherited conventions (*E,* 263–64). Their education and their environment did not hinder their mental and spiritual development, for they were no longer reared to be artificial nonentities (*E,* 136–39, 85–86, 131–32, 400, 263–64). Although Bellamy complimented the serious, original, and thoughtful women reformers of the nineteenth century by attributing to their success the women of the year 2000, he also wrote that their program had been too narrow and limited because they had misinterpreted the true cause of the tyrannical treatment of females. Instead of blaming "tyrant man" or "man the monster," the women should have recognized that the whole social system had been at fault and that the primary cause of their slavery had been an economic one that had been banished by economic equality (*E*, 133–35).

Courtship and Marriage

Since by economic equality women were now liberated from having to marry in order to survive, Bellamy placed upon them great responsibility for the welfare of the human race and its development. Long before *Looking Backward* and *Equality*, he had written in his journals, manuscripts, and newspaper publications about the fetters marriage placed upon both men and women and about the fact that, since women relied upon the capture of a husband for economic security, they used their beauty and their wiles to "shackle him." In fact, opined Bellamy, the girls who so desperately needed a husband to support them regarded men as horses which, if captured, could be ridden; and they looked upon men's taste for women as an angler regarded a fish's for worms—as a foolishness of which they could take advantage.[88]

In an 1875 review of L. B. Walford's *Mr. Smith* he commented that the book presented an excellent picture of feminine pettiness and coquetry when matrimonial designs were afoot; and he concluded that the moral of the work was that the coquette was as contaminated morally as the women of the demimonde were physically.[89] In his journal of the same period he wrote about the love of an "utter woman" who loved and thought of no concealment but who was not wise enough to enhance her gift of love by bestowing it in driblets or by employing the coquettish arts which would have brought the man she loved to his knees. In the unpublished manuscript "The Medium's Story" Bellamy portrays Grace as rebelling at the convention that forces her to disguise the depth of her love until after marriage; and in "Pott's Painless Cure" he portrays the deceits of courtship practiced by both men and women.[90]

Bellamy was opposed to loveless marriages that were made for economic or social reasons because they interfered with the working of Darwin's theory of natural selection and because women, if they were not to be a torment to themselves and others, should marry those they loved—and so should men if they sought sympathy, companionship, and helpfulness from their wives.[91] Although Bellamy wished people to marry only because of love and their mental and spiritual sympathies, he realized that the rich did not always

marry the rich for monetary reasons, that lovers had other responsibilities to consider besides fulfillment of their desires, and that
prudence had to be considered relative to other factors. Realizing
the differences that education made in true companionship, Bellamy
recognized cultural inequalities as a barrier to marriage; but he
maintained that making an ado over the marriage either of a Christian to a non-Christian or of a Caucasian to a Negro was an "unchristian . . . notion." Such intermarriages had best be left to the
taste of the concerned individuals.[92]

Since marriage involved the welfare of a lifetime and since "the
gloss of the early passion gilded at best only the first few months
of marriage," Bellamy advised that practical consideration be given
not only to comfort but to heredity. Individuals who had mental
or physical diseases or who had indulged in debilitating drugs and
stimulants were to forego marriage, for no man or woman had the
right "to transmit a hereditary taint to posterity."[93] When Charles
Darwin proposed that legislation be passed that would prohibit
marriage of the deaf, the dumb, the insane, and the tubercular,
Bellamy doubted that a law would prevent such alliances; and he
advocated that the best method would be to create an intelligent,
reasonable public attitude that would cause the afflicted to have a
"moral sentiment" about being bound by duty to humanity to be
celibate.[94]

In 1873 and 1875 Bellamy informed the readers of the *Union*
that stirpiculture was considered favorably by scientists, and he
applauded the farmers who at a convention had discussed "one of
the greatest social questions of the time," human breeding. He cited
the farmer who had said that, since scientific mating of cattle was
successful, it should be tried with human beings. In this same
editorial Bellamy admitted, however, that humanity would in all
probability never conform to any other reasons for marriage than
"sentiment, passion, and policy."[95] However, he outlined a story
about a future society in which the government regulated matrimony
and procreation for the improvement of humanity. The system to
be used to regulate citizens was an enlightened form of stock raising:
it employed the principles of crossbreeding advanced by the "writers
on temperament."[96]

In *Looking Backward* Bellamy repeated his adverse criticism of
courtship as a constrained, artificial relationship between the sexes;
and he instituted an equality in wooing which, because of the

woman's economic equality, made it possible for her to declare her love, maintain her modesty, and dispense with the coquetry and affectation despised by the citizens of the year 2000 (*LB*, 217, 250). In "A Love Story Reversed" (1888) Bellamy delineated this new system by portraying the modesty of the heroine who found the man she loved, told him of her love, won him for her husband—and found him grateful; for, he admitted, he might never have found the woman that God had intended for him if she had not declared her love.[97]

Love is portrayed in *Looking Backward* as being quicker in growth, more quickly and frankly acknowledged, and the sole moral basis of marriage (*LB*, 247, 215–16). Bellamy expected Darwin's theory of natural or sexual selection, which he regarded as essential to the betterment of humanity, to influence the "physical, intellectual, and moral character of the race."[98] Despite his advocacy of natural selection, Bellamy somewhat limited the freedom of the future citizens: they are taught to have a moral responsibility for the future race, and this ethical concept so reinforces their sense of duty that they select only the best and the noblest of mates (*LB*, 219). Bellamy provided two suggestions about how this moral sentiment could be made effective: women were to be reared to regard themselves as the guardians of the world to be, and they were to have a "sense of religious consecration" (*LB*, 220). As a result, any woman who betrayed the future welfare of the citizens by marrying a male who had not acquitted himself "creditably in the work of life" would defy the opinions of other women who had obeyed and who had believed in the selection of the best and noblest as husbands (*LB*, 219–20).

In *Looking Backward* Bellamy portrayed a world in which economic problems did not affect homes, the use of leisure, or parenthood; for every child was provided economic security from the cradle to the grave. Parents had, however, the responsibility of discovering the capabilities of their children and of being good parents (*LB*, 213). Although some Malthusian critics thought his granting economic equality to all members of a family would lead to overpopulation and starvation, Bellamy answered them in the *New Nation* by citing the fact that the rich and cultivated families of the nineteenth century did not have numerous offspring; and, since the citizens of the ideal state would have widened thoughts and interests, these diversions would decrease their sexual impulse. In fact, the energy and passion formerly expended in sexuality would be directed toward the general advancement and elevation of the human type and toward an investigation of the spiritual and the Infinite. Since women would no longer be the sexual slaves of their husbands, they would not become mothers unwillingly; and their natural instinct of self-preservation would cause them to limit the number of children.[99] Besides these factors, the progress being made in the mechanical and chemical sciences, such as hydroponics, would so increase the production of foods that an increase in the population would not cause any serious problems.[100]

In *Equality* Bellamy not only repeated the answers he had given to the Malthusians (*E, 410–12*) but also said more about the sexual code and the food supply of the year 2000. In describing the sexual ethics resulting from the new status of women and from economic equality, he stated that the moral principle on which sex was based was that the first condition of ethical action in any relationship was the freedom of the actor (*E, 140*). Sexual relationships only became moral ones, therefore, when women became independent and were not forced by economic dependence to marry a man who could support a wife and family. To Bellamy, marriage in the nineteenth century had really been an economic contract in which the man legally assumed the task of supporting his wife and his children; and the whole moral code had been based on whether or not sexual unions were legal—not upon whether they involved persons unfitted to have progeny or whether they were inspired by sordid motives. When women had indulged in illicit sexual relationships, they had been considered unchaste and abandoned no matter how great their love had been; but men who had enjoyed such sexual relationships had fared much better because they had enjoyed the double standard they had created.

In the year 2000 one standard of conduct was observed: all men and women had to face each other with "attitudes of absolute equality and mutual independence." Mothers no longer had to teach their daughters to protect themselves from their own generous instincts, and no one could acquire any sexual proprietorship that could be asserted and maintained against the will of another. Since each person was to have "absolute sexual autonomy and independence" as a result of economic equality (*E, 408*), women no longer assumed the names of their husbands when they married; and their children assumed, according to sex, the surname of the mother or the father (*E*, 139).

Other Innovations

To free women for their role as contributors to the nation, Bellamy provided other innovations that would ease life not only for women but for all citizens. He defined in his editorials and book reviews many of the concerns that led to innovations in *Looking Backward* and *Equality* concerned with safe housing, the preservation of the countryside, the beautification of cities, the convenient serving of food, the wearing apparel, and the cultural life. As might be expected, Bellamy was also greatly concerned about the health, happiness, and safety of people. He sought by his innovations to improve both their settings and their lives.

When Bellamy reviewed Sir Arthur Help's *Social Pressure* in 1874, he noted that the main theme of the book was that the small towns and the rural areas should be so improved that they would have the advantages of the cities and that metropolitan areas would be so planned that they would provide the advantages of country life.[101] In *Looking Backward* Boston is portrayed as a city of broad streets, open squares, parks filled with fountains and statuary, beautiful public buildings, and houses set in broad gardens or yards (*LB*, 27). Since the houses are heated and the public conveyances are operated with electricity (*LB*, 30), the city lacks the noise and dirt of the nineteenth century which, in his nightmare, Julian compared to an inferno (*LB*, 265). Bellamy observed in the *New Nation* that a rapid transit system would permit the citizens to live outside the cities.[102] The whole tendency of Nationalism was to check the growth of cities at the expense of the country; for, since central control of production and distribution would destroy the advantages that the cities had had over towns, decentralized industry and population would result.[103]

In *Equality* Bellamy expanded the statements he had made in the *New Nation* by depicting the transformation in the cities and the countryside that would result from Nationalism. The growth of cities had been halted by nationalization of the industrial and merchandising systems, since the need of labor and commodity exchanges that had made the cities so popular among laborers and producers no longer existed. People who had been drawn to the cultural advantages of the city now lived in the country, where they had the same public conveniences from which they could quickly travel to the cities when they so desired. Since all citizens could afford equally good housing and could choose where they would live, many of them left the cities because they preferred the charms of the countryside—and this move happened despite the fact that city people lived in low, comfortable houses located among groves of trees. Because of the telephone and the electroscope, the inhabitants of the mountains and the countryside could enjoy at home concerts, theatrical productions, and lectures (*E*, 292–95).

Bellamy had had very little to say in *Looking Backward* about the type of houses in which people lived, but he had stated that citizens selected their residences on the basis of their needs and tastes and that they paid the state a stipulated but graduated rent. Although the houses were simple and comfortable, the public buildings and the country and town clubhouses of the guilds were magnificent (*LB*, 85–86, 126–27, 255; *E*, 292–93, 295, 371). Bellamy advised readers of the *New Nation* that homes and industrial buildings would be so planned, located, and built that they would insure the safety and health of the inhabitants.[104] In his descriptions of the structure and furnishings of the houses in *Equality*, Bellamy evinced his continued concern about the health of citizens: houses were so well-built and in such good repair that no catastrophic fires occurred; interiors had such hard, durable surfaces that the rooms could be cleaned by spraying from a hose; and, since the dwellings were heated with electricity, they were more comfortable and less dirty than those of the nineteenth century (*E*, 51).

In these improved homes the furnishings—carpets, bedding, draperies, dishes, pots and pans—were made from paper,[105] and they were replaced instead of being cleaned or washed when they were soiled. The discarded furnishings were returned to the factories, where the material was recycled and made into other articles. The result of these innovations of the year 2000 had been the eradication of the germs of contagious diseases, and that in turn had contributed more than any other change to the increased health of the citizens (*E*, 51–53). Shoes, women's slacks and dresses, and all other garments were made of paper by factories which did not follow designs established by Paris or New York but fulfilled the individual desires of the citizens.

During the years 1874 to 1881 Bellamy wrote several articles commenting on the benefits of cooperative means of minimizing household chores and of increasing social pleasures, and he also indicated that great savings could be the result of cooperative dining places.[106] He introduced in *Looking Backward* public kitchens and public dining halls which contributed to freeing women from the kitchen. Though the citizens ate their two minor meals of the day in their homes, food was delivered to them by pneumatic tubes from the public kitchens. The major meal of the day was consumed in the beautiful public dining hall where, for a small fee, the family could rent its own dining room. Each family had to order its main meal a day in advance from the menu that listed what would be available, and the food ordered could be as elaborate or as simple as the family members desired (*LB*, 116, 123–24). The waiters who served in the public dining hall were well-educated young men in the general labor force; and, since they were the social equals of those they served, they were treated as such (*LB*, 123–27).

Needless to say, Bellamy's plan for such service that replaced the laborer in the private kitchen aroused the interest of women,[107] and he outlined in "A Vital Domestic Problem" (1889) in *Good Housekeeping* the method women could use to organize public laundries, cooperative agencies for cleaning, and public kitchens. He indicated that municipal ownership of such public services would be the first step toward household reforms that would make women the true mistresses of their homes and not the slaves in them.[108] Bellamy repeated in *Equality* the value of such cooperative enterprises, but he stressed the benefit of public, scientific cooking; of the international menu that had been accumulated; and of the "new food materials and the new methods of preparing them" discovered by the botanists and chemists (*E*, 289).

Although cooperative laundries did not exist in *Equality* because of the use of paper clothing, the citizens of the year 2000 enjoyed free water, light, news, operas, concerts, plays, libraries, postal and electrical communications, excellent roads, and rapid transit lines. Beautiful natatoriums were also open day and night, as were all of the public services because the citizens had day and night shifts during their years of service. Whenever they worked and wherever they lived, the people of the ideal state were able to enjoy equally well and according to their individual tastes the facilities, comforts, and amusements that were provided for their happy living and diversion.

The Effect of the Social Order

When some politicians dubbed Bellamy's followers as the "salvation army," he wrote in the *New Nation* that he accepted the title because he truly wished to "offer men salvation from the earthly hell of poverty, with the physical wretchedness, the mental darkness, and the morally degrading surrounding which it implies."[109] He realized that men and women would have to be freed from their materialistic concerns by having their physical needs satisfied; for only when such comfort was achieved could they devote themselves not only to art and culture but to intellectual and spiritual development.

Chapter Five

The Influence of Edward Bellamy

There is no denying the wide influence of Edward Bellamy. *Edward Bellamy Abroad* (1962) describes the impact of *Looking Backward* and *Equality* in other countries. Bellamy's ideas affected some of the most important American novelists of his era—William Dean Howells, Ignatius Donnelly, and Albion Tourgee—and led to the writing of utopian novels that supported or rejected his ideas. A thorough study should be made of the many others who were greatly impressed, as they admitted, by his concepts: Charles Beard, Eugene Debs, Hamlin Garland, Mark Twain, Edmund Bok, Winston Churchill, William D. Lloyd, Ida Tarbell, Jack London, Upton Sinclair, William Allen White, Stephen Leacock, James Turner, Richard Ely, Carl Sandburg, Vernon Parrington, Frank Lloyd Wright, Walter Foss, Louis Adamic, Henry Elmer Barnes, Heyward Broun, and Thorsten Veblen. Many of these people were interested in Bellamy's ideas; and some were involved with movements such as Nationalism, Populism, and Christian Socialism that were very important influences in the nineteenth century and even later. It is through a study of these movements that the pervasiveness and the controversiality can be best identified.

Nationalism and Populism

The founding of the Nationalist Club movement has been briefly described in chapter 1. The history of such organizations may be divided into two periods: during the first stage, 1888–1891, the clubs devoted themselves primarily to a moral crusade, to publications, and to the education of their members; in the second stage, 1891–1896, the Nationalists entered the field of political action as the important supporters and contributors to the People's Party or Populists.

During the first period, the Boston Bellamy Club appointed a committee of five—Sylvester Baxter, Cyrus F. Willard, General A. F. Devereux, Captain Charles E. Bowers, and the Reverend W. D. P. Bliss—to prepare a plan for their organization.[1] Since the document, presented on 9 January 1889, not only was adopted by the Boston club but was used by other clubs organized throughout the country, it deserves quotation:

The principle of the Brotherhood of Humanity is one of the eternal truths that govern the world's progress on lines which distinguish human nature from brute nature.

The principle of competition is simply the application of the brutal law of the survival of the strongest and the most cunning.

Therefore, so long as competition continues to be the ruling factor in our industrial system, the highest development of the individual cannot be reached, the loftiest aims of humanity cannot be realized.

No truth can avail unless practically applied. Therefore, those who seek the welfare of man must endeavor to suppress the system founded on the brute principle of competition and put in its place another based on the nobler principle of association.

But in striving to apply this nobler and wiser principle to the complex conditions of modern life, we advocate no sudden or ill considered changes; we make no war upon individuals; we do not censure those who have accumulated immense fortunes simply by carrying to a logical end the false principles upon which business is now based.

The combinations, trusts, and syndicates of which the people at present complain demonstrate the practicability of our basic principle of association. We merely seek to push this principle a little further and have all industries operated in the interest of all the nation—the people organized—the organic unity of the whole people.

The present industrial system proves itself wrong by the immense wrongs it produces; it proves itself absurd by the immense waste of energy and material which is admitted to be its concomitant. Against this system we raise our protest: for the abolition of the slavery it has wrought and would perpetuate, we pledge our best efforts.[2]

By the second anniversary of the Boston Bellamy Club, other clubs had been rapidly formed in the east and had mushroomed on the West Coast as well. After April 1889 the New York club had been formed; and others had been organized in Washington, D.C.; Hartford, Connecticut; Chicago; Portsmouth, New Hampshire; Brooklyn, New York; Zanesville and Cincinnati, Ohio; Minneapolis; St. Louis; Philadelphia; and Baltimore. In California sixty-two clubs with a membership of over three thousand people existed by June 1890. Nationalism had "put the silk hat"[3] upon socialism, for club members included lawyers, journalists, editors, writers, artists, doctors, ministers, and businessmen. As Cyrus Willard had advocated, these were not "the weak, crying for mercy, they were the strong, demanding justice. They were not the crank or uneducated foreigner, importing ideas declared to be 'exotic'; they were the men of position, educated, conservative in speech. . . ."[4]

By December 1889 Cyrus Willard could state that fifty newspapers and magazines unreservedly advocated Nationalism,[5] and Mason Green reported in 1890 that he could visit the editorial rooms of every leading New York or Boston newspaper and shake hands with a Nationalist.[6] Among the Nationalist publications were the *True Commonwealth*, Washington, D.C.; the *Boston Commonwealth;* the *Alliance-Independent*, Lincoln, Nebraska; the *Pittsburg Kansas;* the *Altrusian*, Columbus Junction, Iowa; the *Coming Nation*, Greensburg, Indiana; the *True Nationalist*, New York City; the *Commonwealth*, New York; the *Altruist*, St. Louis; the *Star*, Richmond, Virginia; the *Progressive Age*, Minneapolis; *Unity*, Chicago; and the *Living Issue*, Cincinnati. By 1890 seven newspapers in California had been founded or were supported to express Nationalist principles: the *Pacific Union*, a labor paper that became converted to Nationalism; the *Abolitionist*, a weekly published by Rabbi Samuel J. Freder of San Francisco; the *Weekly Nationalist*, the official organ of the California Nationalists which succeeded the *California Nationalist;* and the *Kaweah Commonwealth*, the publication of the Kaweah Community which had been founded in 1886 to employ the principles established in Gronlund's *Co-operative Commonwealth.*[7] Other California newspapers that proclaimed themselves Nationalist were the *Cactus*, the *Pacific Monthly*, and *Looking Forward.*[8]

In December 1889 Cyrus Willard suggested that all the Nationalist clubs of Massachusetts should become centers of "practical politics" and seek the election of state representatives.[9] The Nationalists of the state had introduced a bill in 1889 that would permit municipal ownership of gas and electric lighting plants; although the bill was defeated in the legislature of 1889–90, it was passed in 1891. In the following year sixteen towns in Massachusetts and several in Ohio began to establish municipal lighting plants.[10] As noted earlier, public ownership of utilities was one of the initial steps in the development of Bellamy's ideal state, one which he believed would awaken people to the values of collective ownership. The first political victory of the Nationalists had occurred.[11]

Bellamy's publication of the *New Nation* introduced the second stage of the Nationalist movement—political action in support of the Populists. But he also stated quite clearly that he did not "believe that the nationalistic clubs, as organizations, should turn themselves into campaign clubs. The clubs stand for more advanced principles than any party is likely at once to take up, and it would be unwise policy for them as clubs to engage in any line of work which would compromise the completeness of their doctrine. But individually and as citizens, we hope and believe that nationalists generally will be found in sympathy with the new party."[12]

As an individual, Bellamy had his own reasons for supporting the Populists. The first was his statement in the "Prospectus" of the *New Nation* that the publication "will criticize the existing industrial system as radically wrong in morals and preposterous economically, and will advocate the substitution therefore, as rapidly as practicable, of the plan of national industrial co-operation, aiming to bring about the economic equality of citizens, which is known as nationalism."[13] He also sought to bring the various reform groups and labor organizations into closer accord so that they could have the power to secure legislative reform.[14]

An April 1891 article in the *New Nation* announced that the Nationalists had been invited to attend a convention in Cincinnati on 19 May, 1891, for the formation of the Third Party.[15] When the chairman of the platform committee, Ignatius Donnelly, welcomed the Nationalist delegates, he greeted Mason Green and his colleagues with the words "Edward Bellamy—whom not to know is to argue one's self unknown."[16] As William Dean Howells remarked, Bellamy had "virtually founded the Populist Party,"[17] for its platform owed much to the ideas expressed in *Looking Backward* and in the *New Nation*. The platform finally presented at the Omaha convention in July 1892 indicated the importance of the comment about Bellamy by Donnelly, who was primarily responsible for its contents,[18] contents that Bellamy found Nationalist in spirit and language.[19] In fact, he informed the Nationalists that Populism had "the largest opportunity yet presented in the history of our movement to commend it to the masses of the country. If we fail to take the utmost possible advantage of it, we shall make a fatal mistake."[20] For the first time in his life Bellamy played an active role as a citizen and a publisher in supporting a political party.

In the *New Nation* and in his speeches, Bellamy explained the particulars of the Populist platform. In an address at a public meeting of the party at Faneuil Hall, Boston, on 17 October, 1891, he commended the Populists for their intention to carry popular government into industry, a necessity if the republican form of government was to survive.[21] He addressed the Populist convention at Faneuil Hall on 30 March, 1892, when representatives to the Omaha convention were selected. Bellamy was chosen to be the Chicopee Falls delegate. When Bellamy was expected to address the ratification meeting of the party ticket that was held at Tremont Temple on 13 October 1892, he was unable to attend because of illness; but, in the letter he sent to be read to the three thousand attendants, he stated that the People's Party was a means of attaining the American dream of a true republic of equality, fraternity, liberty, and justice and of saving the republic from the rule of industry.[22]

The Cincinnati-Omaha platform contained many of the ideas that Bellamy had expressed as interim or initial means of attaining his ideal state. It advocated the extension of the powers of the central government; government ownership of the railroads, telegraph, and telephone; civil service for all government employees; government postal savings banks; and the popular election of United States senators.[23] Although the Nationalists approved what some considered a very radical platform, the 1,654 delegates, who were "white and black, native and naturalized, lettered and unlettered, professors, farmers, artisans, doctors, newspaper men, women, and a millionaire,"[24] accepted it; and General James B. Weaver of Iowa was nominated for president.

During the Omaha convention the Nationalists established their own committee for propaganda work; they hoped the committee would eventually include a representative from each state and formulate a powerful national committee to circulate petitions to Congress in support of legislation for the purchase of the nation's telegraph and telephone facilities. Mason Green acted as general secretary and E. S. Luscomb as corresponding secretary for the committee, which tried as late as 1893 to perfect a national organization.[25] From 1893 to March 1898 the Nationalists had their own Bureau of Nationalist Literature in Philadelphia which distributed Bellamy's speeches, *Looking Backward,* and Professor Frank Parsons's "Public Ownership of Monopolies" and "Philosophy of Mutualism." By October 1897 the bureau had distributed over 104,000 copies of its publications. The bureau closed when B. Franklin Hunter, who had had it in charge, resigned from his regular employment in the post office to join the Ruskin Colony.[26]

In the election of 1892 the Populist's General Weaver received 1,065,191 votes; he had carried six states; and he had twenty-two votes in the electoral college—the first time since the Civil War that a third party had won such votes.[27] In the states the Populists elected three governors, three state senators, and seventeen representatives.[28] A twenty-five percent increase in 1893 had occurred in Iowa, and progress had also been made in Virginia, Ohio, Colorado, and Nebraska.[29] In Massachusetts the vote of the Populists trebled. But Bellamy was indignant because "a conspiracy of silence" had led to articles in the Boston papers about the decline of the party: the regulation dispatches from the polls—prepared by the Western Union Company and by the New England Press Association—provided no space for the recording of the Populist vote. As a result, the gains made by the Populists were ignored. In the congressional election of 1894 the Populist vote increased forty percent.

Because of the votes generated by the Populists, the Republican and Democratic parties began to adopt planks from their platform. When the Populists joined the Democrats in 1896 and William J. Bryan, the hollow-headed but silver-tongued orator, ran on the free-silver issue for president of the United States, Bellamy and many of the Nationalists were not only disappointed about Bryan's selection but did not approve of his issue. As a result of the merger with the Democrats and then of the Spanish-American War of 1898, the Populists as a party faded away. However, the effects of *Looking Backward* lingered; for other Bellamy movements occurred intermittently in the United States; and many Nationalists continued to be active in public affairs, with the Christian Socialists, or as founders or participants in other organizations.

Christian and Other Socialists

Before and after the decline of the Nationalist and the Populist movements, many of Bellamy's followers had had their own allegiances with different church groups and with socialism. In February 1889 the clergymen associated with the Boston Bellamy Club founded the Christian Socialists, at the instigation of Reverend W. D. P. Bliss, an Episcopal minister who believed ecclesiastical unity was a means of social reform, and Reverend Francis Bellamy, a cousin of Edward and a Baptist. This organization included many ministers of different denominations: the first president was the Reverend O. P. Gifford, a Baptist; and the vice-presidents were Mary A. Livermore, a Universalist, and the Reverend Philo W. Sprague, an Episcopalian. Very shortly after their first meeting the Christian Socialists founded the monthly magazine the *Dawn: A Magazine of Christian Socialism and Record of Social Progress,* with Bliss as editor; it had as its motto "He works for God who works for man."[30]

The principles of the Christian Socialists were succinctly stated in the *Dawn* and reprinted in the *New Nation:* "Christianity without socialism we believe to be a lie; socialism without Christianity we consider a fatal mistake."[31] Bliss wrote to Bellamy in April 1889: "I agree fully with your idea that what we need is not goody, goody church-talk, but plain advocacy of what to do. And I also agree with you that whatever we call it what we want is Nationalism, and none of our Christian Socialists think of withdrawing from that movement; we simply want to aid it by rousing the church for Nationalism."[32] To Bellamy, Christian Socialism differed from Nationalism only in that the latter had "greater definiteness and completeness in its program" and that the former stood upon theological premises whereas Nationalism was "logically derived from humanitarian" principles.[33]

Despite Bliss's statement to Bellamy about support of Nationalism, the Christian Socialists criticized the Nationalists at times in articles in the *Dawn* for not having affiliated with the laborers' organizations, for not being concerned about unemployment problems, and for having advocated in *Looking Backward* and in Nationalism not an evolutionary but a static situation.[34] Although Bliss attempted to interest other cities and churches in establishing Christian Socialist organizations, he was not very successful. But he maintained his efforts to formulate a nationwide organization by a lecture tour of the Middle West in 1890. As a result, societies were founded in Chicago and Cincinnati, and the Kansas State Christian Socialist Society was organized by the Reverend Harry C. Vrooman. Still, the Christian Socialist movement had dissolved by the end of 1890, and the *Dawn* published nothing about its activities.

Although Bliss was forced to leave his position with the Grace Church of South Boston, he continued to publish the *Dawn* "in the interest of social Christianity." He eventually founded in Boston the Mission of the Brotherhood of the Carpenter, which in 1890 led to the creation of a group united in supporting practical Christianity.[35] By 1891, Bliss had rented a large house to serve as a community center for Christian Socialist fellowship and as the headquarters for the Brotherhood, as well as for meetings by all sorts of reform groups, discussion groups, and labor unions. After the Christian Social Union was organized in New York City in 1891 under the auspices of the Protestant Episcopal Church in order to promote the study of social and industrial questions and to arouse interest in them,[36] Bliss became a member, as did the Reverend J. O. S. Huntington.

Before Bliss took a lecture tour for the Christian Social Union, he was convinced that the solution to social and economic problems was the People's Party. But after his discussions with the party leaders during his travels, he decided that little political change could occur. As a result, he lost interest in political movements: he had decided that the country needed a great spiritual awakening before anything concrete could be accomplished. While visiting England in 1894, Bliss became deeply impressed by the aims and educational achievements of the British Fabians. Early in 1895 he not only had founded the American Fabian League but had established the *American Fabian,* a magazine that continued publication until 1900. Although the nationwide league that Bliss had envisioned and attempted to organize never materialized, many independent, unorganized Fabians continued to read his publication. Next Bliss undertook the founding of the ineffective National Education and Economic League, which was to serve the workers and their unions; the Union Reform League, whose members were mostly Christian Socialists; and in 1901 the publication *Social Unity.*[37]

Because of his ambition and his sincerity, Bliss was from 1889 to 1896 a speaker for most of the "radical Protestant churchmen"; and his organizations of one kind or another appealed to various prominent individuals. His disciples included the Reverend George Herron, founder of the religious, radical magazine the *Kingdom,* who sponsored the cause of the Populists and who in 1899 became a Socialist; and Walter Rauschenbusch, a Baptist minister and a professor of church history, who in 1889 founded the newspaper *For the Right* and who later wrote such books as *Christianity and the Social Crisis* (1907), *Christianizing the Social Order* (1912), and *The Social Principles of Jesus* (1916). Rauschenbusch, who had also read *Looking Backward,* urged the adoption of an industrial democracy because he regarded capitalism as anti-Christian; he announced in 1892 that Populism was the Christian approach to politics; and, in 1900, he—like many others—became the supporter of Eugene Debs, a candidate for president of the United States.[38]

Debs had been suggested as candidate for president in 1896 by Henry Demarest Lloyd and other Populists irked by and fearful of the leadership of the ambitious Populists, who were selling out to the Democrats and supporting Bryan. But, although Debs had been impressed by the ideas of Bellamy's *Looking Backward* and by Gronlund's *The Co-operative Commonwealth* (both of which he had read while in prison) and was also a Populist, he preferred to give speeches in support of Bryan. After the decline of Nationalism and Populism, Debs became interested in the organization Brotherhood of the Cooperative Commonwealth, and he planned to create a colony based upon its principles in the state of Washington to solve the problems of the unemployed of the American Railway Union. At a meeting in Chicago in 1897, the Brotherhood group withdrew from the plans that Debs had presented. Its spokesman, Fabian Frank Parsons, indicated that no group would be supported that did not have the broad membership and the ideals of the Nationalists.

As a result of this meeting, Social Democracy was created, with the aim of restoring "land and all the means of production, transportation, and distribution, to the people as a collective body."[39] Social Democracy supported not only public employment of the unemployed but also the colonization program Debs desired. Because of the split in the party over political action and colonization, the meeting in 1898 ended with the majority voting for colonization; and, as a result, the minority immediately founded the Social Democratic party with Debs as one of its leaders. When this party met in Indianapolis in March 1900 more than 4,500 members attended from 236 branches of twenty-five states.[40] Although the platform of the party ignored the farmers and the blacks, Daniel Bell has quite clearly indicated that it contained some Populist items that were later endorsed by the New Deal.[41]

Professor Daniel De Leon of Columbia University, who had left the Nationalist movement in order to found the Socialist Labor party in 1890, criticized Debs because his "element held to the Utopian idea that votes would be enough to overthrow capitalism."[42] But some of that group left the Socialist Labor party in 1900 and selected their own candidates for president and vice-president at their convention. Later this same group joined the Social Democratic party, and a united Socialist party ticket nominated Debs for president and Job Harriman as vice-president. Although difficulties were to continue after the merger of the two parties, the popular vote for Debs was almost three times that for De Leon.[43]

Although the Socialist party had its Golden Age from 1900 to 1912 and although Debs was almost consistently selected until World War I as a presidential candidate, it was always bothered by internal squabbles about political action and religion. By 1919 fifty-six percent of the membership was foreign-born, and many leaders and members deserted in order to support the New Freedom of Woodrow Wilson, who had attacked the monopolies and the control of the government by Big Business. When the party denounced the entrance of the United States in World War I, it was eventually dissolved by the Espionage Act of 1917; mailing rights for Socialist publications were suspended, the party's national offices in Chicago were raided, and many of its officers were indicted for opposing conscription.

The Theosophists

Thomas Wentworth Higginson wrote about *Looking Backward* that it created "a band of young proselytes who, instead of believing that what he [Bellamy] says is too good to be true, believe that it is too good not to be true; and are ready to proclaim its teachings as at least a temporary gospel of good news."[44] Among the first to be appreciative of Bellamy's novel were two members of the Theosophists, Sylvester Baxter and Cyrus Willard. Baxter wrote for the *Boston Herald* the first long, appreciative review of *Looking Backward*,[45] and Willard stated in his critique in the *Boston Globe* that his thinking had been so affected by Bellamy's utopia that it had crystallized his view about the possibilities of cooperation.[46] As has been noted, these two Boston journalists sponsored the formation of the first Boston Bellamy Club that other Theosophists joined; among them were Henry Willard Austin, Arthur B. Griggs, George D. Ayers, John S. Cobb, and George Ranson Bridge.[47] Willard stated in his unpublished autobiography that he and Baxter were interested in "the new society" because of the "pervading spirit of *Looking Backward*" : "Universal brotherhood, a dominant element of Theosophy."[48]

Six of the seven founding members of the Boston Bellamy Club were Theosophists (the seventh was Bellamy). When the *Nationalist* began publication, one of its first editors was John S. Cobb, who— with Madam Blavatsky, William Judge, and Colonel Henry S. Olcott—was one of the original founders of the Theosophical Society in New York in 1875. When Cobb had to surrender editing the publication, Henry W. Austin assumed his position, but the responsibility soon devolved upon Cyrus Willard.[49] In an article about the Boston Bellamy Club published in the *Nationalist* in May 1889 Willard recalled that the club had sent "forth an influence which has moulded the other clubs now springing up like the army of Cadmus—Cadmus who sowed the dragon's teeth and who also taught Greece her letters. . . ." Shortly before the *Nationalist* began publication in May 1889 Bellamy received a letter from one of the founders of the Theosophical Society, William Q. Judge, an Irish lawyer, requesting that Bellamy submit an article to *Path,* the Theosophist publication which he edited. To Judge, "Nationalism . . . is, as you know, founded on the principle of Universal Brotherhood. I thus conceive of it as closely linked to Theosophy, and a desirable means whereby Theosophists may assist in the ethical advancement of the race, substituting brotherhood and cooperation for competition, and do good work on the practical plane."[50]

As Arthur Morgan, Bellamy's biographer, makes clear, the Theosophists were very active in Nationalist clubs in New York, Chicago, and California; and, according to the account of Abbott B. Clark, the California clubs were organized because of the praise given *Looking Backward* in H. P. Blavatsky's *The Key to Theosophy* (1889). As a result, "the Nationalists Clubs in California sprang up all at once in towns and cities where there were branches, as we called them, of the Theosophical Society. We all knew that it was a spontaneous action of Fellows of the Theosophical Society that organized the Nationalist Clubs." What in Bellamy's novel had so attracted the Theosophists, according to Clark, was "the absence of 'class consciousness.' " Emphasis was placed upon the "transition of the nineteenth-century condition to the ideal state without class conflict, hate or injustice. It seems to me that this point cannot be overemphasized."[51]

Arthur Morgan and Clark have stated that the Theosophists dropped their interest in Nationalism when its members became politically involved with the Populists.[52] This was not universally true. Cyrus Willard, a Theosophist, became in 1897 a member of the Socialist party when it was organized; he was one of the commission employed to promote the practical application of "industrial co-operation as exemplified in *Looking Backward* ";[53] and he assured Bellamy and the other "old boys in the Nationalist movement" that his work was "only the continuation and realization of the movement."[54] Willard's commission published its own section in Debs's paper the *Social Democrat;* and, in 1898, when the second *New Nation* was published, Debs and Willard were listed as contributors.

The Crucial 1930s

In 1929 the Utopian Society of America, Incorporated, was founded as a secret organization in California, where the Bellamy organizations had always flourished. The society supported "an end to private ownership, the establishment of a priceless, profitless system, production for use, and the creation of a great cooperative commonwealth with only those between the ages of twenty-five and forty-five called to work, and that for only a few hours each day." In 1934 the Utopian Society held a mass meeting that filled the Hollywood Bowl. When the organization was at its height, it had purportedly a membership of 600,000 to 750,000 members in the clubs that existed in seventeen states.[56]

When Upton Sinclair, who had published *The Jungle* (1906) and his *Industrial Republic, A Study of the America Ten Years Hence* (1907), created his End Poverty in California (EPIC) league and ran in 1934 for governor of the state, the Utopian Society gave him its whole-hearted support. When Sinclair was not elected, the society lost prestige. Although doubts existed about Sinclair's knowledge of Bellamy's utopian novels and about his Nationalism, he had had for many, many years three important Nationalists as his friends:

Richard Otto, the wealthy founder of the Long Beach Bellamy Society and Sinclair's later political campaign manager; H. Gaylord Wilshire, the Nationalist candidate for Congress in 1890 and the publisher of *Wilshire's Magazine,* which sponsored government ownership; and Julius A. Wayland, the Indiana-born-and-reared journalist who became a Kansas Nationalist and who published for many years the *Coming Nation* and then the *Appeal to Reason,* which by 1900 had the largest subscription list of any newspaper in the world.[57] Wayland promoted the ideas of Bellamy, Gronlund, Henry Demarest Lloyd, and Debs; and he frequently republished "The Parable of the Water Tank." Moreover, he was the good friend of Sinclair who, when all other publishers had rejected *The Jungle,* published it as a serial in the *Appeal to Reason.*

In a letter of 24 July 1958 Sinclair wrote that he was "a Bellamy fan and *Looking Backward* was one of the first books on Socialism I read. Also it was one of the first books I gave to my wife when I met her; it converted her, and she says if it hadn't she wouldn't have married me. . . . Bellamy later wrote an economic study— the name has slipped my mind—as good as anything I ever read. A really sound book, too little known."[58] In "A Utopian Bookshelf," Sinclair stated that *Equality* made him wonder how many knew that Bellamy had followed his best-seller with "one of the wisest and most comprehensive economic studies ever produced?" To Sinclair, this second utopian novel contained "more meat for this time than it did fifty years ago. 'Looking Backward' is a story which will hold your interest and at the same time start trains of living ideas in your mind. If you will follow it up by reading 'Equality' you will understand how a collectivist society can be democratic, humane, and free. . . ."

In 1938 the All States Bellamy Association of Los Angeles sought to coordinate the programs of the different clubs. As a result of this effort, the association distributed bulletins that advocated reforms and also copies of *Looking Backward.* In 1941 fifteen clubs and study groups existed in California.[59] A comparable Edward Bellamy Group had been founded in April 1932 in Brooklyn, New York; it became the Edward Bellamy Association of New York in 1933. Its purpose was similar to that of the All States Bellamy Association: it desired to establish local chapters throughout the United States and to maintain communication with those at home and abroad. The honorary members of this group included Heywood Broun, journalist and critic; Harry Elmer Barnes, historian, editor, and educator; John Dewey, philosopher, educator, and author; and Mrs. Edward Bellamy.[60]

During the Great Depression articles about Bellamy appeared in many newspapers and magazines, some of them written by prominent Americans. Ida Tarbell, the famous muckraker, included Bellamy in "New Dealers of the Seventies" (*Forum,* September, 1934). Gilbert Seldes, journalist, drama critic, and former editor of the *Dial,* published "True to Type" in the *New York Evening Journal* (28 October 1933), noting that Bellamy's "system of distribution of labor and of its rewards . . . seems . . . far less impossible than the promise of Eugene Debs seemed in 1916." Heywood Broun considered Bellamy "America's most authentic prophet" ("It Seems to Me," *New York World Telegram*); but, when he wrote the introduction to the Modern Library edition of *Looking Backward,* he stated that it "should be measured more by its influence than by its prophetic accuracy." And John Dewey, in "A Great American Prophet" (*Common Sense,* April 1934), wrote that Bellamy had "grasped the human meaning of democracy as an idea of equality and liberty." The June 1933 issue of *Golden Book,* a monthly magazine that reprinted stories and articles from world literature, published Bellamy's solution for unemployment under the title "A Solution for Unemployment Devised in 1893 for the Present Crisis"; and it reprinted in October 1934 "The Parable of the Water Tank." In 1933 *Looking Backward* was republished as a serial in the *Boston Post.*

During this same period two other movements influenced by *Looking Backward* and *Equality* received much attention: the Townsendites and the Technocrats. Dr. Francis Townsend, a retired physician who had been working with an agency that aided the poor, introduced a plan to aid the aged whose savings had disappeared and who could, for many reasons, find no work. The plan, the result of Townsend's having read *Looking Backward,* was published in the *Long Beach Press-Telegram* in September 1933 and proposed that individuals over sixty be given an income of $150 a month—one which they would be required to spend in order to create a demand for jobs for the younger population. The article generated a controversy that led Townsend to circulate petitions; several thousand signatures were obtained; Townsend asked his friend Robert Earl Clements to become his aide; and on 24 January 1934, Townsend and Clements filed for incorporation of their organization, Old Age

Revolving Pensions, Ltd. By August of the same year Clements began organizing clubs, and by January 1935 Clements and Townsend were publishing *Townsend National Weekly,* which had within a year more than 200,000 subscribers.

In January 1935 Congressman John S. McGoarty, who had been elected with Townsend's support, introduced in the House of Representatives a bill endorsing a $200 income each month for all citizens over sixty if they would spend the money within thirty days and if they were not gainfully employed. Because of the millions that the Townsend Plan would have cost the government—roughly half of its income for one-eleventh of its population—and because the Social Security Act had also been introduced, Townsend's proposal was viewed with skepticism by members of the New Deal. The proposal was not passed by the Congress, but many members spoke highly of Townsendism as an extraordinary social-political movement. Despite its popularity, it did not get the support of Upton Sinclair's EPIC. Still, the political forces the Townsendites had gathered may have caused faster passage of the Social Security Act.[61]

The Technocrat organization, founded by Howard Scott, evolved into many diverse groups: the Continental Committee on Technology, the American Technocratic League, and the Utopian Society of America, founded in California by the engineer Eugene J. Reed. Although all of these groups advocated the reading of *Looking Backward* and *Equality* and were ideologically related to Bellamy's views, the one that announced a plan most clearly derived from his utopias was the Continental Committee on Technology. This group sponsored the acquisition and control by the state of natural resources and industry, the appointment by the state of skilled technicians, and the use of the products for the benefit of all citizens. Every citizen had to contribute his services in order to aid the cooperative industries in meeting the needs of all citizens; but such enterprise was not only to improve the standard of living but to provide the leisure that would permit the development of personal interests.[62] In Denver the American Technocratic League used the term "industrial democracy," sponsored production for the benefit of the citizens, and urged democratic control of the type that had been sponsored by the Socialists and by Bellamy.[63] Although the organizations for technocracy prospered during the Great Depression, they differed too much, were not very certain about their objectives, were too inefficient to survive, or were incapable of stressing Bellamy's improved morality as a preparation for and as a result of the ideal state.

Among the many organizations that were formed in the 1930s, the Bellamy-inspired ones differed greatly from those interested either in Fascism or in Marxism—an interesting but frightening story related by Arthur M. Schlesinger, Jr., in *The Age of Roosevelt, The Politics of Upheaval* (1960). Schlesinger describes such radicals as Father Coughlin, who attracted both Catholics and Populists, and Huey Long (who was reared in Winn Parish, Louisiana, a Populist center), who organized the Share Our Wealth Society in 1934. Long proposed a homestead allowance of $5,000 and an annual income of $2,000, as well as other benefits: limitation of the hours of labor; government storage and control of agriculture and production; a pension for every citizen over the age of sixty; and college education at the expense of the government.

Although Long's ideas paralleled those expressed by Bellamy, he was less respected by the radicals than Alfred Bingham, a well-educated New Englander, who founded in 1932 *Common Sense,* a magazine that sponsored radical discussions, and who also wrote *Insurgent America: Revolt of the Middle-Classes* (1935). In his book Bingham urged a technocratic society that would produce for use only, its citizens thereby rendering service to self and the rest of the population. When "production-for-use" had proved its superiority, the "old system would be gradually drained away, and it would be left an empty shell. A transition to an economy of abundance would have been effected."[64] In the introduction to his book Bingham noted that such a future state had already been outlined; for *"Looking Backward* (1888) and *Equality* (1897), remain the best full-length description of such an economic system."

In *Common Sense* Bingham, other editors, and contributors consistently praised Bellamy. Charles Beard and John Dewey, like Bingham, had great respect for his ideas. To Beard, "Bellamy's epic dream served as a torch from which were lighted the aspirations of multitudes in the United States"; and, to Dewey, "the Worth of Bellamy's books in effecting a transition of the ideas of democracy into economic terms is incalculable. . . . Bellamy's work is definitely constructive. While it is filled with fundamental criticisms of the present anarchy . . . It accords with American psychology in breathing the atmosphere of hope."[65] During its life, from 1932 to 1946, the writers published in *Common Sense* included such famous Americans as John Dos Passos, Upton Sinclair, Louis Adamic, Archibald MacLeish (who also published *Public Speech,* in which he sponsored collectivist thought), Norman Thomas, and Max Eastman.

Although no precise record exists of the influence of these movements on the innovations of the 1930s, two of the famous leaders of this period—Norman Thomas and Franklin D. Roosevelt—were well acquainted with Bellamy's concepts. Like other ministers of the 1890s and the 1930s, Thomas, who in 1918 began to edit the publication the *New World* (later the *New World Tomorrow*), resigned from the ministry. He became an active member of the Democratic Socialists because of the poverty of his East Harlem parish and his opposition to World War I. Like other Socialists of America, Thomas rejected the Marxist concept of revolutionary methods, for, like Bellamy, he preferred the evolutionary process for attaining public ownership of production and services. Thomas stated that he had read Bellamy's *Looking Backward* and "was much impressed by it long before I became officially a Socialist. . . . I did not read *Equality* until after I was a Socialist. By then I often referred to both books and especially to the *Parable of the Water Tank.*"[65] When Eugene V. Debs died in 1926, Thomas became the leader of the Socialists. He ran for various offices—governor of New York, mayor of New York City, and, like Debs, many times for president of the United States.

Thomas's most important roles were his fight for civil liberties, his work with the farmers and the labor unions, and his many books and impressive speeches. Because of the factions that existed among the Socialists, they never achieved the political power that unity might have given them; but Thomas's methods for helping the citizens stricken by the Great Depression of the 1930s revitalized interest in Socialism and also contributed to the New Deal. Thomas advocated public works for the unemployed, minimum wage laws, the shorter work week, unemployment insurance, the end of child labor, and government responsibility for the welfare of the economy.[66] During this period of economic stress, Thomas published four books and many articles in which he stressed not only the need for a cooperative commonwealth as the solution of the Great Depression but also the fact that doomed capitalism had to be replaced by democratic collectivism.

Needless to say, Thomas was at first resentful that many Socialist ideas had been adopted and implemented by the New Dealers. He was most critical of their lack of concern about "basic moral issues in the face of immediate economic problems" and also their "lack of overall conceptualization." Later he was less angry at what the New Deal had accomplished, for it had "constituted something like a revolutionary change in American attitudes and policies. It established a welfare state and strengthened democracy."[68] Thomas eventually withdrew from socialism as a political party; he proposed, as had Socialists before him, that energy be spent instead in educating the American people. When he reread *Looking Backward* in the 1960s, Thomas recorded in *Socialism Re-examined* (1963) that, "once deeply impressed" by it, "Now I know that men could live in his Utopia with far less happiness than he imagines would follow from its admirably just economy. . . . I crave a map of Utopia in my atlas which I cannot draw to my own satisfaction." In the same passage Thomas stated that no improved situation could be the result of violence; it had to be created by citizens with vision, and the challenge was to create an organization that would also provide "the true freedom of the individual."[69]

Franklin Delano Roosevelt and his wife were acquainted with the books of Edward Bellamy. But Mrs. Roosevelt stated that, "while both my husband and I were familiar with Edward Bellamy's books and discussed them at various times in small groups of people, I really have very little knowledge of the effect that they had on other people." Although she stated that her husband was "always receptive to new ideas and loved to discuss them," she did not feel that Bellamy had had any effect upon him.[70] Irving Flamm, a lawyer and the author of *An Economic Program for a Living Democracy* (1942), was impressed by the presence of *Looking Backward* in the "most conspicuous part of one of the bookcases in the library" of the White House when he toured it in 1933. Flamm, who had been "a Bellamy fan for some forty years after reading his two volumes" and who had distributed many copies of *Looking Backward,* said that seeing the book in the White House library had intrigued him about its possible influence upon Roosevelt because, in part, of "the caption of his own later book, *Looking Forward*" (1933).[71]

Whatever the specific influence of Bellamy's ideas during the New Deal, the fact is that many of them, sponsored by so many Socialists and Bellamy-related organizations, were implemented; and some of Roosevelt's influential staff members were well acquainted with such proposals. Arthur Morgan, Chairman of the Board of Directors of The Tennessee Valley Authority and a biographer of Edward Bellamy, was a believer in an "integrated social and economic order" that would be achieved as a result of "the democratic process of voluntary general agreement."[72] According to Morgan, Adolf A. Berle, Jr., the assistant secretary of state and a respected member of the New Deal group, was the son of a man who had been an active member of the Boston Bellamy Club and was reared in a family in which *Looking Backward* was comparable to the family Bible.[73] According to Berle, Jr., "It is unnecessary to say that any one who ever followed Bellamy could ever remain uninfluenced by his ideas."[74]

Among the agencies established during the New Deal for the administration of its policies were the Agricultural Adjustment Association (A.A.A.), the Civilian Conservation Corps (C.C.C.), National Recovery Administration (N.R.A.), Works Progress Administration (W.P.A.), and the Tennessee Valley Authority. These agencies sponsored such programs and policies as the use of unemployed youth to replant forests and the hiring of unemployed adults to redecorate the schools and to do other work needed by the nation. Legislation was passed to benefit not only the farmers but the laborers; trade unions were recognized; the minimum wage and maximum hour law was passed; the irrigation system was publicly owned; submarginal lands were removed from cultivation; the soil conservation program was inaugurated; more protection was given workers from the hazards of industry; public control of water power and electricity was initiated; and social security and unemployment insurance were inaugurated. The Supreme Court was liberalized, needy children were given free books and lunches, and laws were established to protect investors. As Arthur Morgan and Everett W. MacNair have made clear, other policies sponsored by Bellamy in the *Nationalist* and the *New Nation* in the 1890s have been inaugurated: low-cost housing; free school textbooks; compulsory school attendance; free manual training and physical education courses; free federal recreation projects; health insurance; free public parks, libraries, and art galleries; voting rights for women; parcel post; graduated income and inheritance taxes; parity commodity loans to farmers; the increase of the school year beyond twenty weeks; the

direct election of senators; the merit system in civil service; and
initiative and referendum.[75]

As a result of the thinking of Edward Bellamy and the action of
those influenced by him, the ideas of *Looking Backward* and *Equality*
never died. They led to evolutionary reforms that greatly modified
the capitalistic system of the nineteenth century. That ideas sponsored by Edward Bellamy are still coming to pass has just been
reproved by the Labor Department's recent announcement that it
has developed a "free, computerized national 'Help-Wanted' list"
matching "unemployed Americans with Job Openings."

Because of the joblessness created by technocracy, computers, and
robots, more highly educated and accomplished workers are going
to be needed; as Bellamy stated long ago, they have to be prepared
to fill many different jobs in the course of a lifetime. The broadly
educated and better-trained populace that Bellamy desired to provide
for the socioeconomic benefit of his country and for the development
of individuals is today a greater necessity, for Americans in this
present period of transition must, as Bruno Bettelheim has suggested, not only live the good life but also "create anew in each
generation the good society for himself and all others." Like Bellamy, Bettelheim believes that man "must be equipped to change
society so that it will not be an obstacle to living the good life, but
a setting that facilitates and encourages it."[76] As the thinking and
dreaming of Edward Bellamy have proved, individuals may inspire
others and bring about change. Oscar Wilde once stated, "A map
of the world that does not include Utopia is not worth even glancing
at, for it leaves out the one country at which Humanity is always
landing. And when Humanity lands there, it looks out, and, seeing
a better country, sets sail. Progress is the realization of Utopia."[77]

Notes and References

Books and articles written by Edward Bellamy are cited without his name. Unless otherwise noted, all Bellamy materials—notebooks, manuscripts, and letters—are deposited in the Bellamy's collections of the Houghton Library, Harvard University. Anonymous works are cited as "Anon." The signed works by authors other than Bellamy are fully identified.

Chapter One

1. Lillian Symes and Travers Clement, *Rebel America* (New York, 1934), 131; Mrs. Clam Skeele Palmer, *Annals of Chicopee Street* (Springfield, Mass., 1879), 6–7; and Sumner Van Horn, "Chicopee Years Ago," *Springfield Republican*, n.d., clipping in collection of Connecticut Valley Historical Association, Springfield, Mass.

2. Notebook XI, 23.

3. "Overworked Children in Our Mills," *Springfield Union*, 5 June 1873.

4. Thomas Hughes, "Prefatory Memoir," *Alton Locke* by Charles Kingsley (London, 1878), xxxi.

5. Joseph Bellamy, quoted in Arthur Morgan, *Edward Bellamy* (New York, 1944), 215–16.

6. [Clark W. Bryan], "Editor's Portfolio," *Good Housekeeping* (December 1889), 95.

7. Marion Bellamy Earnshaw, daughter of Edward Bellamy, interview with author, Springfield, Mass, 18 October 1950.

8. Morgan, *Edward Bellamy*, 22.

9. Earnshaw, 25 October 1950, interview with author.

10. Mason Green, "A Biography of Edward Bellamy," Bellamy MSS., 12.

11. Earnshaw, 25 October 1950, interview with author.

12. Letter of Maria Louise Putnam Bellamy to Mrs. E. H. Gorham, Bellamy MSS, 1181 (108–10), n.d.

13. Green, "Biography," 12.

14. Charles Bellamy, lawyer and publisher, was also a novelist who, like Edward, was critical of the social-economic situation and a Utopian. His best-known works are *The Breton Mills* (1879), *The Way Out* (1884), and *An Experiment in Marriage* (1889).

15. According to Bellamy's wife, Emma Sanderson Bellamy (20 October 1950, interview with author), Bellamy discussed more things of a serious nature with his mother than with anyone else.

16. Green, "Biography," 9; see also Morgan, *Edward Bellamy*, 53.

17. Folder XIX (1874).

18. Ibid.

19. Ibid.

20. Green, "Biography," 28–29.

21. Edward Bellamy, Interview, *Free Press Telegram*, n.d., n.p.; Bellamy family clipping file possessed by Marion Bellamy Earnshaw, Springfield, Mass.

22. Letter of Paul Bellamy to Arthur Morgan, 8 May 1940; Morgan MSS, Houghton Library, Harvard.

23. "Home, Sweet Home," *Springfield Union*, 27 September 1873, 4.

24. Notebook II, 1874 (?).

25. Folders VII and II.

26. Green, "Biography," 16.

27. Letter of Mrs. Rufus King Bellamy to Harriet Putnam Packer, 20 December 1866 or 1867(?).

18. "Necessary Self Education," Folder VII, 1–2.

29. Notebook XI (188?), 12.

30. Frederick Bellamy, speech to Bellamy Club of Boston, 29 March 1916.

31. Letter of Edward Bellamy to Council of Delta Kappa Epsilon, Aug. or Sept., 1887.

32. Earnshaw, 20 October 1950, interview with author.

33. "A Positive Romance," *Blindman's World* (Boston, 1898), 290. This story was written in 1889.

34. Letter of Isaac Landt.

35. Frederick Bellamy, speech, 2; Morgan, *Edward Bellamy*, 369.

36. "How I wrote 'Looking Backward'," *Ladies Home Journal* 2 (April 1894): 2.

37. Green, "Biography," 23.

38. Eliot Carson, Notebook XI (188?), 13.

39. Green, "Biography," 22; Notebook II (188?), 15.

40. "A Friendly Criticism," *New Nation*, 7 November 1891, 645.

41. "Woman Suffrage," *Golden Age*, 11 March 1871, 3.

42. Letter of William S. Packer, September (1871).

43. Green, "Biography," 30.

44. "Railroad Disasters," *Golden Age*, 18 March 1872, 2; "National Education," *Golden Age*, 30 March 1872, 2.

45. Notebook XV (188?), 17.

46. Letter of Mr. and Mrs. Rufus King Bellamy, 21 May (1872), to Edward Bellamy.

47. Folder I, First Lyceum Talk (1870?), 8–9.

48. Second Lyceum Talk (1871 or '72), 6, 15.

49. Notebook I (1871–'74), 38–39.

50. Notebook I (1872), 28–29.

51. "With the Eyes Shut," *Blindman's World*, 347–48.

52. Notebook XIV, 74–75; Notebook III, 217–18.

53. Notebook II, (1870), 57–58.

54. Notebook B (188?), 14.

55. Notebook I, 30–32.

56. Notebook I (1871–74), 4–5.

57. Eliot Carson, Notebook XI (188?).

58. Notebook V (188?), 7.

59. *The Religion of Solidarity* (Yellow Springs, Ohio, 1940), 43. See also Morgan, *Edward Bellamy*, 200–03.

60. Folder IX, "The Dual Life," 6–7.

61. Folder IX, 6–7, 10–11.

62. Folder XIV, "The very fact that. . . ," 26.

63. Folder XIV, 12–13.

64. Folder IX, "The Dual Life," 10–11.

65. Folder IX, 12–13.

66. Notebook A (188?), 15–16. See also Notebook XIV [187?], 105–6, and Notebook V (1884), 6, 10–11.

67. Notebook V (1884), 12.

68. Notebook IV (187?), 24.

69. Folder IX, "The Dual Life," 1–6.

70. Notebook II (1870?), 48.

71. Folder XXVII, "The Spring Feeling," 15, 1–2.

72. Folder XVI, Fragment beginning "They seem to come forth. . . ," 2.

73. Notebook IV (187?), 3.

74. Notebook II (187?), 52–53.

75. Folder XIV, The very fact. . . , 13.

76. *Religion of Solidarity*, 32–33.

77. Notebook XIV (187?), plot 1.

78. *Six to One* (New York: G. P. Putnam's Sons, 1878), 154; hereafter cited in the text as *SO* followed by page number.

79. "Pott's Painless Cure," *Blindman's World*, 161.

80. Statement of Mrs. Edward Bellamy and of Marion Bellamy Earnshaw, October 1950, to author.

81. "How I Wrote 'Looking Backward,' " 2.

82. Notebook VII (189?), 16–17.

83. *Springfield Union,* 17 June 1873, 2.

84. *Springfield Union,* 2 July 1873, 6.

85. *Springfield Union,* 23 July 1873, 6.

86. Letter of Edward Bellamy to W. D. Howells, 21 August 1881, Howells MSS, Houghton Library.

87. [Anon.], "The Daily News for 1881," *Daily News,* 27 January 1881, 4.

88. [Anon.], *Daily News,* 20 October 1880, 2.

89. Clipping, obituary of Charles J. Bellamy, 12 December 1910.

90. Ibid.

91. Letter of Edward Bellamy to W. D. Howells, Howells MSS, Houghton Library.

92. Hawaiian Notebook (1878), 7–9.

93. Notebook II (1870), 12.

94. "How I Wrote 'Looking Backward,' " 2.

95. "Two Days' Solitary Imprisonment," *Blindman's World,* 106.

96. *Dr. Heidenhoff's Process* (London: William Reeves, n.d.), 139; hereafter cited in the text.

97. Letter of Alice Stone Blackwell to Mrs. Marion Bellamy Earnshaw, 14 December 1933, Bellamy Family Files. Blackwell cites her mother's statement in her book about her grandfather's role in Shays' Rebellion and her view in her autobiography that Bellamy's serial was the only accurate interpretation of the causes of the affair.

98. *Miss Ludington's Sister, A Romance of Immortality* (Boston: James R. Osgood & Co., 1884), 17; hereafter cited in the text.

99. The materialized-spirit concept was probably based upon the Katie King incident in Philadelphia, which Bellamy had written about in "Recent Miracles," *Springfield Union,* 11 August 1874, 6. However, he had also reviewed novels in 1877 and in 1875 that used the same ideas—Gautier's *Spirite* and Marryatt's *Open Sesame.*

Chapter Two

1. Letter of Edward Weeks to author, 29 August 1958.

2. Louis Boudin, "A Marxian Looks at America, This Un-American Movement," *Our America* (January, 1933), 1–2.

3. Sylvia E. Bowman, *Edward Bellamy Abroad* (New York, 1962), 34–35; Bowman, *The Year 2000* (New York, 1958), 93, 104, 105, 314, 315.

4. Review, Professor Crocker's *The Theistic Conception of the World,* "Literary Notices," *Springfield Union,* 23 October 1875, 6.

5. Ibid.

6. *Looking Backward* (New York: D. Appleton and Company, 1933), 107; hereafter cited in text as *LB* with page number.

7. [Anon.], "Declaration of Principles," Nationalist Club [pamphlet] (Baltimore, 1892), 1.

8. "The Progress of Nationalism in the United States," *North American Review,* CLIV (June 1892), 746.

9. [Anon.], "Declaration of Principles," 1.

10. " 'Looking Backward' Again," *North American Review,* CL (March 1890), 354.

11. "Extension of the Municipal Functions the Cure for Municipal Misrule," *New Nation* 2 (9 April 1892):226.

12. Ibid.

13. *Equality* (New York, 1933), 333; hereafter cited in text as *E* with page number.

14. "Programme of Nationalists," *Forum,* 17 (March 1894):84.

15. "Programme of Nationalists," 84; see also *Equality,* 330; "Why Every Workingman Should be a Nationalist," *New Nation* 3 (15 April 1893):193.

16. "Nationalism Logically Implied in Individualism," *New Nation* (13 February 1892):98.

17. "What Nationalism Means," *Contemporary Review* 58 (July 1890):1–18.

18. Lawrence Gronlund, *The Cooperative Commonwealth in Its Outlines: An Exposition of Modern Socialism* (Boston, 1884), 135.

19. Morgan, *Edward Bellamy,* 257.

20. "Principles and Purposes of Nationalism," "Address at Tremont Temple, Boston, on the Nationalist Club's First Anniversary, December 18, 1889" (Philadelphia: Bureau of Nationalist Literature, n. d.), 1–12; reprinted in the *Nationalist* 2 (April 1890):174–80.

21. *Talks on Nationalism* (Chicago 1938), 176.

22. "The Old Faith and the New," *Springfield Union,* 3 December 1873, 2.

23. Notebook XVII, 124, 82, 127.

24. Notebook I (1872), 34.

25. C. J. Bellamy, *The Way Out,* 1–5.

26. "What Nationalism Means," 12.

27. "Plutocracy or Nationalism—Which?" Address of Edward Bellamy at Tremont Temple, 31 May 1889, Nationalist Extra No. 1. (Boston: Nationalist Club of Boston, n.d.), 1–12.

28. "Why Every Workingman Should Be a Nationalist," *Building Trades Council Souvenir,* reprinted in *New Nation* 3 (15 April 1893):193.

29. "Has the Republic Failed?" *New Nation* 2 (27 August 1892):544; "Programme of Nationalists," 81.

30. "Mr. Bellamy's Letter," *New Nation* 1 (21 March 1891):118.

31. "Equality" MSS, "Father, you're a great tease. . . ."

32. "Programme of Nationalists," 82; "Has Nationalism Failed?"
544.

33. "Mr. Bellamy's Letter," 118.

34. *New Nation* 1 (17 October 1891):597.

35. "Programme of Nationalists," 54; Introduction to *Socialism: The Fabian Essays* (Boston 1894), xii–xiii.

36. "Christmas in the Year 2000," *Ladies Home Journal* 3 (January 1895):6.

37. "The Millionaire or the Republic Must Go," *New Nation* 2 (6 January 1892):432–33.

38. "The Globe Away Off," *New Nation* 2 (20 February 1892):115.

39. "Programme of Nationalists," 21.

40. " 'Looking Backward' Again," 354.

41. "Brief Summary of the Industrial Plan of Nationalism . . . for Class Study," *Dawn* 1 (September 1889):3.

42. Cf. Bellamy's speech, "The Cradle of Liberty Rocked," *New Nation* 1 (17 October 1891):506–8.

43. "How and How Far Panics Can Be Prevented," *Springfield Union* 3 October 1873, 4.

44. "Springfield Shylocks," *Springfield Union*, 3 January 1873, 2.

45. "What Nationalism Means," 1–18; "Introduction," *Socialism: Fabian Essays,* xv–xviii; "The Scientific Basis of Economic Equality," *New Nation* 2 (18 June 1892):388–89.

46. "Mr. Gladden Attacks the Principle of Economic Equality," *New Nation* 3 (29 April 1893):216.

47. "Why Should Not the Functions of the Government 'Include Support of the People'?", *New Nation* 3 (15 April 1893):192; "Two Ways of Looking at It and the Right Way," *New Nation* 3 (1 April 1893):166. *Equality,* 78; *Talks on Nationalism,* 409–10; "What Nationalism Means," 10.

48. "What Nationalism Means," 8.

49. *Duke of Stockbridge* (New York, 1900), 77, 26, 344.

50. "Morbid Criticism," 4.

51. Ibid.

52. Notebook II, "Political Views," 1.

53. "Morbid Criticism," 4.

Chapter Three

1. Folder XXIV, "Notes on *Looking Backward,*" 1–3.

2. "Brief Summary of the Industrial Plan of Nationalism," 3; *Looking Backward,* 229–32.

3. Folder XXIV, "Notes on *Looking Backward,*" 1, 4–5.

4. Letter of Edward Bellamy, 20 June 1889; T. W. Higginson MSS, Houghton Library.

5. Folder XXXVII, "Unused Preface to *Equality*," 12–13.

6. Notebook II (1874?), 95, 29–30; Folder XXI, "To Whom This May Come"; "The Old and the New," *Springfield Union*, 23 October 1873, 4.

7. Folder XXXVII, "Unused Preface to *Equality*," 10–11.

8. Notebook XV (1898), 2; "Literary Notices," *Springfield Union*, 29 April 1876, 6; Ibid., 3 April 1874, 6. In these and other instances Bellamy discusses Carlyle, Taine, and the French Revolution.

9. "Woman Suffrage," *Springfield Union*, 25 November 1872, 2.

10. Folder XXXVII, "Unused Preface to *Equality*," 10–11.

11. Notebook XV (188?), 51.

12. "Now Is the Accepted Time," *Springfield Union*, 1 October 1873, 2; August 22, 1877, 4.

13. See also "Principles and Purposes of Nationalism," 12.

14. See also "General Significance of the Events at Homestead," *New Nation* 2 (5 August 1892), 497–98.

15. "Father Trask and His Class," *Springfield Union*, 28 January 1875, 4; "A Non Sequitur," 15 February 1873, 2; "Literary Notices," ibid., 16 February 1876, 6; "Some Good Words Spoiled," 22 June 1876, 6.

16. Notebook IV (187?), 12; "Looking Forward," 2; Folder V.

17. Folder XXVIII, "Some Mistakes of Social Reformers," 1.

18. "Looking Forward," 1–4.

19. Letter of Edward Bellamy, 28 December 1888, T. W. Higginson MSS, Houghton Library; Folder XXVIII, "Some Mistakes of Social Reformers," 1.

20. Ibid.

21. "Not Too Soon," 49.

22. Letter of Edward Bellamy, 28 December 1888, T. W. Higginson MSS, Houghton Library; "Not Too Soon," 49.

23. *Equality* MSS, chap. 25, 6.

24. *Springfield Daily News*, 14 January 1881, 2; "Touching Things Spiritual," *Springfield Union*, 17 November 1875, 4.

25. Letter of Edward Bellamy, 28 December 1888, T. W. Higginson MSS, Houghton Library.

26. Letter of Bellamy to Yates, 6 April 1889, Massachusetts State Historical Society Library, Boston.

27. "Progress of Nationalism," 750; "First Steps Toward Nationalism," 181; "The Piece-meal Process," *New Nation* 1 (28 January 1891):695.

28. "Nationalism and the Liquor Question," *New Nation* 1 (20 June 1891):326; "Disastrous Effects of Impure Liquors Which Public Management Would Prevent," *New Nation* 2 (2 July 1892):418; "How We Shall Get There," *Twentieth Century* 2 (11 May 1889):167; "First Steps Toward Nationalism," 174–81; "Programme of Nationalists," 87; Bellamy letter to Yates.

29. Letter of Bellamy to Yates; "Principles and Purposes of Nationalism," 7–8.

30. Letter of Bellamy to Yates; "How We Shall Get There," 167.

31. "The New York Standard Suspends," *New Nation* 2 (10 September 1892):567.

32. "Principles and Purposes of Nationalism," 8–10; " 'Looking Backward' Again," 9; "First Steps Toward Nationalism," 183–84; "Why Workingmen Should Favor All Propositions for Public Operation of Business," *New Nation* 2 (11 March 1893):129–30.

33. "Programme of the Nationalists," 88–89; "Principles and Purposes of Nationalism," 9; "First Steps Toward Nationalism," 183–84.

34. "How We Shall Get There," 187.

35. "Principles and Purposes of Nationalism," 10; Folder XXVII, "An Iowa Subscriber."

36. "Is Nationalism Reconcilable with a Wage System" *New Nation* 2 (12 March 1891):161; "The Editor and the Office Boy," ibid. 2 (7 February 1891):29.

37. E. E. Hale, *Sybaris and Other Homes* (Boston, 1869), 53; Lewis Mumford, *The Story of Utopia* (New York, 1941), 155; Richard Ely, *French and German Socialism in Modern Times* (New York, 1883), 68, 69.

38. General Francis A. Walker, "Mr. Bellamy and the New Nationalist Party," *Atlantic Monthly* 65 (February 1890):248–62; William Morris, " 'Looking Backward'," *Commonweal* 5 (22 June 1889):194–5.

39. "Talks on Nationalism," 265.

40. "How I Wrote 'Looking Backward'," 2.

41. See also "Literary Notices," *Springfield Union*, 2 October 1875, 6.

42. "Earning Before Spending," *Springfield Union*, 15 November 1873, 4; "The Ethics of Strikes," 15 April 1873, 2.

43. "What Nationalism Means," 12; *Looking Backward*, 47, 158–59.

44. *New Nation* 2 (30 July 1892):481.

45. Bellamy letter cited in "The Great Principle Involved at Homestead," *New Nation* 2 (20 August 1892):532.

46. "The Right to Labor. Work for the Unemployed. What Can and Ought to be Done," *New Nation* 2 (2 January 1892):18–20. See also "The Solution and the Only One of the Unemployed Problem," ibid., 3

(9 September 1893):417–18; interview from *Boston Traveller* reprinted in "Should the State or Municipality Provide Work for Its Unemployed," ibid., 3 (11 November 1893):493–94; "What Ought to be Done for the Unemployed," ibid., 3 (16 December 1893):530; "The Cooperative Solution of the Unemployed Problem Here Fully Set Forth," ibid. 4 (20 January 1894): 25, 27; "A Solution for Unemployment Devised in 1893 for the Present Crisis," *Golden Book Magazine* 17 (June 1933):48–49.

47. "The Policy of Public Work in Dull Times," *Springfield Union,* 21 November 1874, 4.

48. Ely, *French and German Socialism,* 112; Rev. E. Kaufmann, *Utopias: or Schemes of Social Improvement from St. Thomas More to Karl Marx* (London, 1879), 143–45.

49. Symes and Clement, *Rebel America,* 140.

50. "City Industries," *New Nation* 1 (14 February 1893):38.

51. Notebook XVII (187?), "Blackstone Commentaries," 51.

52. Folder XIX (187?), "An Essay at Autobiography," 19–26; Notebook II (187?), 14–15.

53. Folder VII (1863), "The Force of Flattery," 1; Notebook II (187?), 14–15.

54. Notebook I (October 1872), 32–34.

55. "Pott's Painless Cure," *Blindman's World,* 167, 174. See also "Taking a Mean Advantage," "Hooking Watermelons," "Echo of Antietam," "To Whom This May Come."

56. Bellamy cited by S. Baxter, "What Is Nationalism?" 12.

57. "More Talk about 'Individualism' and Common Sense," *New Nation* 3 (1 April 1893):167; *Equality,* 321.

58. "Talks on Nationalism," *New Nation* (14 March 1891):111.

59. *Looking Backward,* pp. 74–5, 101; "Talks on Nationalism," *New Nation* 1 (14 February 1891):37.

60. "Talks on Nationalism," *New Nation* 1 (14 March 1891):111.

61. "Talks on Nationalism, *New Nation* 1 (14 February 1891):37.

62. "Some Account of Eugene Richter's Anti-Socialistic Romance," *New Nation* 3 (3 June 1893):275; *Looking Backward,* 100.

63. " 'Looking Backward' Again," 312–13; "Talks on Nationalism," *New Nation* 1 (4 July 1891):111; (14 February 1891):37.

64. "The Question of Incentives Once More," *New Nation* 1 (18 April 1891):189; "Talks on Nationalism," ibid. 1 (27 June 1891):346; *Equality,* 35–6; "What Nationalism Means," 5.

65. "What Nationalism Means," 4; "Talks on Nationalism," *New Nation* 1 (21 June 1891):346; "Cut Bait or Fish," ibid. (14 March 1891):110; " 'Looking Backward' Again," 357; "The Question of Incentives," 189.

66. "What Nationalism Means," 4–5.

67. Ibid.

68. Letter to Bellamy from Mrs. Frances E. Russell, Chairman of the Committee on Dress, National Council of Women of the United States, 30 October 1893.

69. "A Continuation of Our Friendly Debate with Professor Secretain," *New Nation* 1 (21 November 1891):678.

70. "Talks on Nationalism," *New Nation* 1 (18 April 1891):192.

71. Frances E. Willard, speech at the Woman's National Council, Washington, D.C., 22 February 1891, cited in *New Nation* 1 (14 March 1891):102.

72. Mary A. Livermore, "Cooperative Housekeeping," *Chautauquan* 6 (April 1886):396–98. See also Mrs. Abby Morton Diaz, "The Why and the Wherefore," *Nationalist* (December 1889), 5–10; Mary H. Ford, "A Feminine Iconoclast," *Nationalist* (November 1889), 352–57.

73. "Literary Notices," *Springfield Union*, 4 December 1875.

74. "Medical Education in the United States," *Springfield Union*, 8 November 1875, 4.

75. Walker, "Bellamy and the New Nationalist Party," 248–62.

76. Cited in Lewis Mumford, *The Story of Utopias* (New York, 1941), 138.

77. Notebook, "Thoughts on Political Economy," 13 August 1867, 1–4; Folder IX, "Political Views," 2.

78. Notebook, "Thoughts on Political Economy," 10–14.

79. "The Compensations of Elections," *Springfield Union*, 28 October 1876, 4.

80. "Taking the Election," *Springfield Union*, 15 November 1876, 4.

81. "The Compensations of Elections," 4.

82. "Morality and Politics," *Springfield Union*, 17 November 1876, 2.

83. *Springfield Union*, 16 March 1877, 7.

84. "New Books," *Springfield Union*, 12 July 1873, 2.

85. "The Logic of the Situation," *Springfield Union*, 10 March 1877, 4.

86. *Springfield Union*, 23 October 1876, 6.

87. [Anon.], "Bribery at New York," *Springfield Daily News*, 3 November 1880, 3.

88. "Some Questions Answered," 499.

89. "A Reform Worth Having," *Springfield Union*, 13 July 1876, 2.

90. "The Swedish Civil Service," *Springfield Union*, 21 November 1877, 4.

91. "What Nationalism Means," 13.

92. "Practical Questions about Railroad Nationalization," *New Nation* 3 (2 September 1893):410.

93. "The Illinois Farmers in Convention," *Springfield Union*, 4 April 1873, 2; "The Flow of the Population City-ward," ibid., 7 September 1875, 5; "Real Independence," ibid., 20 January 1877, 5; "Scientific Farming," ibid., 3 November 1875, 4; "Good Reading for Farmers," ibid., 16 August 1876, 4; "Talks on Nationalism," *New Nation* 1, (29 August 1891):490; "The American Farmer Must Choose Between Becoming a Nationalist or a Peasant," ibid., 3 (21 October 1893):466.

94. "Talks on Nationalism," *New Nation* 1 (29 August 1891):490.

95. Ibid. 488–89.

96. "The American Farmer Must Choose . . . ," 466; "Farming Corporations," *New Nation* 2 (11 June 1892):372.

97. "The American Farmer Is Being Turned Into a Peasant," 210; *Equality*, 304.

98. "Farmers, Frost, and Nationalism," *New Nation* 2 (19 September 1891):535.

99. "A Nationalist Text from Calvin's City," *New Nation* 2 (12 November 1892):675.

100. "Principles and Purposes of Nationalism," 5.

101. Folder XVII, "A faith in the good time coming . . . ," 3–4, 5–15.

102. In *A New Constitution for the United States of the World* (New York, 1872) Victoria Woodhull proposed that a league of nations be formulated by revising the Constitution.

103. Folder XVII, "A faith in the good time coming . . . ," 3–4.

104. Ibid., 5–15.

105. Notebook VII (189?), "Certain general consequences of the new order," 57–58.

106. "Devices to Restore Popular Government," *New Nation* 2 (1 June 1892):372; "An Excellent Book on a Very Important Theme," ibid., 2 (23 July 1892):466.

107. "The Case of Boss Tweed," *Springfield Union*, 18 December 1872, 2; "The Arrest of Charles Bowles," ibid., 19 December 1872, 2. "Railroad Disasters," *Golden Age* 2 (16 March 1872):2; Notebook XI (188?), 13–15, 36–40; *Looking Backward*, 164, 168.

108. "The Lynch Law," *Springfield Union*, 2 December 1872, 2; Ibid., 11 December 1872, 2.

109. Folder XVIII, "New York, April 24, 1872," 3–4; "Liberty of the Press," Folder XII, 6–7.

110. *Springfield Union*, 19 December 1872, 2; "Trial by Jury," ibid., 8 February 1873, 2; "An Absurdity of the Jury System," ibid., 6 July 1875, 4.

111. "How to Serve Free and Speedy Justice," *New Nation* 2 (2 July 1892):420; "How Rich and Poor Can Be Equalized before the Law," ibid., 2 (9 July 1892):420; "Let Us Have Free Justice," ibid., 3 (29 April 1893):214–15.

112. "Judicial Reform," *Springfield Union*, 9 January 1877, 2.

Chapter Four

1. Notebook XI (188?), 47–48; Folder V, "This scheme of a future so bright . . .," n.p.

2. Notebook II (187?), 52–53; "Literary Notices," *Springfield Union*, 5 November 1873, 1; *Six to One*, 45–46.

3. Notebook VII (189?), 43–45.

4. "The Religion of Solidarity," quoted in "Edward Bellamy," *Equality*, vi.

5. Folder XVII, "A faith in the good time coming . . .." 1–6.

6. Folder XII, "Liberty of the Press," 35.

7. Folder VI, "Religion," 1.

8. "Literary Notices," *Springfield Union*, 21 April 1877, 6.

9. "Nationalism and Anarchy," *New Nation* 1 (12 December 1891):727; "Talks on Nationalism," ibid., (19 May 1891):239.

10. Notebook I (1871–74), 11–12; "With the Eyes Shut," *Blindman's World*, 347–48; "The Church of the Future according to Matthew Arnold," *Springfield Union*, 8 June 1877, 2; "Christianity as a National Law," ibid., 7 January 1874, 4; "Matthew Arnold's New Gospel," ibid., 7 June 1873, 2.

11. "Puzzles in Morals," *Springfield Union*, 1 June 1875, 2.

12. "How They Look at Him," ibid., 27 January 1877, 5.

13. "Wastes and Burdens of Society," *Springfield Union*, 15 November 1877, 4.

14. "Professor David Swing and the Chicago Presbytery," ibid., 5 May 1874, 4.

15. "A Mischievous Divorce," ibid., 6 November 1875, 4; "Christianity as a National Law," 2; "Christianity and Civilization," ibid., 17 May 1873, 2. See also Notebook II (187?), 33–34.

16. "Christianity as a National Law," *Springfield Union*, 2; "Christianity and Civilization," 2.

17. "Literary Notice," *Springfield Union*, 20 November 1875, 6.

18. "Touching Things Spiritual," 4.

19. "Criminals—Who They Are," *Springfield Union*, 21 December 1872, 2.

20. "Home Types of Wickedness," *Springfield Union*, 21 October 1875, 4.

21. See items listed in n. 10 above; also "Misapplied Charity," *Springfield Union,* 17 February 1874, 4.

22. "Literary Notices," ibid., 8 October 1874, 5.

23. "The Upbuilding Work of the Church," *Springfield Union,* 24 April 1875, 4–5; "How They Look at Him," ibid., 27 January 1877, 4.

24. "Professor David Swing and the Chicago Presbytery," 4.

25. "Religious Services for the Masses," *Springfield Union,* 7 November 1872, 2; "Look on this Picture and on That," ibid., 1 May 1875, 4; "Literary Notices," ibid., 23 September 1873, 6.

26. Notebook II (1878–79), 40–41, 22–23; *The Duke of Stockbridge,* 71, 138, 48–49, 225. "Literary Notices," *Springfield Union,* 21 October 1875, 6, in which Bellamy wrote of Dr. Holland's *Sevenoaks* that the author must have lived in a New England factory town to be able to delineate so well "the servility of the social and ecclesiastical interests to the mill owners or agents,"

27. "Religious Nonsense and Religious Common Sense," *Springfield Union,* 22 November 1872, 4. "Moral and Religious Revivals," ibid., 21 February 1874, 4.

28. "The Minister a Citizen," ibid., 10 April 1875, 4; "Literary Notices," ibid., 12 March 1873, 3.

29. "Literary Notices," ibid., 13 March 1875, 6.

30. "How the Alliance Has Met the Two Great Enemies of Protestantism," ibid., 11 October 1873, 4.

31. "Literary Notices," ibid., 21 October 1873, 6; ibid., 23 September 1876, 6; ibid., 7 January 1874, 6; ibid., 6 December 1873, 6; "The Revision of the Bible," ibid., 3 July 1872, 2.

32. "Why Don't God Kill the Devil," ibid., 28 October 1873, 6.

33. "Literary Notices," ibid., 29 May 1873, 2; 23 July 1874, 4; E. E. Hale, *Sybaris,* 67–68.

34. "Literary Notices," *Springfield Union,* 14 July 1876, 3; 16 December 1873, 6; 31 December 1874, 6; 8 January 1876, 6.

35. "Literary Notices," ibid., 9 September 1876, 6.

36. Ibid., 14 May 1874, 4.

37. "Variety in Unity," *Springfield Union,* 7 October 1873, 4.

38. Anna L. Dawes, "Mr. Bellamy and Christianity," *Andover Review* 150 (April 1891):413–18; William Higgs, "Bellamy: Objections to his Utopia," *New Englander and Yale Review* 52 (March 1890):233; Michael Maher, "Socialists' Dream," *Month* 72 (January 1891):1–9, (February 1891):173–88; A. G. Sedgewick, "Bellamy's Utopia," *Nation* 65 (26 August 1897):170–71; F. A. Walker, "Bellamy and the New Nationalist Party," *Atlantic Monthly* 65 (February 1890):248–62.

39. Bellamy clipping, n. p. December, 1889.

40. "Looking Forward," *Nationalist* 2 (December 1889):2. See also "Talks on Nationalism," *New Nation* (21 February 1891):53.

41. "Christmas in the Year 2000," *Ladies' Home Journal* 12 (January 1895):6; "Talks on Nationalism," *New Nation* 1 (28 March 1891):144.

42. "Christmas in the Year 2000," 6; "The Churches and Nationalism," *New Nation* (3 December 1891):710.

43. "Talks on Nationalism," *New Nation* 1 (21 February 1891):53; "Christmas in the Year 2000," 6.

44. "Concerning Nationalism, the Churches, and the New Political Economy," *New Nation* 3 (13 May 1891):243.

45. Notebook VII (189?), 48.

46. Folder I, First Lyceum Talk, 1–2.

47. Ibid.

48. "National Education," *Golden Age* 2 (20 March 1872):2. "An American Education," *Springfield Union*, 6 March 1875, 4; "A Book on Education," ibid., 13 September 1873, 4.

49. "Statistics of Children," *Springfield Union*, 29 November 1876, 4; "Children in Factories," ibid., 25 July 1872, 2.

50. "Our Unemployed Young Men," ibid., 19 September 1874, 6; "Ignorance and Loaferism," ibid., 28 February 1873, 2; "Compulsory Education," ibid., 8 August 1872, 2; "Our Children Must be Educated," ibid., 24 November 1874, 6.

51. "How Our Girls Are Better Educated Than Our Boys," *Springfield Union*, 7 November 1874, 4.

52. See the items listed above, n. 50.

53. "What Our Young Men Should Resolve to Become," *Springfield Union*, 17 March 1874, 4.

54. "The True Mission of the Teacher," ibid., 3 September 1874, 4.

55. "A Much Needed Educative Reform," ibid., 8 August 1874, 4.

56. "More School Superintendents Called For," ibid., 7 July 1877, 4.

57. "A Much Needed Educative Reform."

58. "What Reading for the Young," *Springfield Union*, 15 August 1877, 4.

59. Bellamy wrote in his review of Professor Bert G. Wilder's *What Young People Should Know* that reading it would solve the mystery of sex that so frequently led to vice; "Literary Notices," *Springfield Union*, 15 May 1875, 6.

60. "Sex in Education," *Springfield Union*, 27 December 1873, 4.

61. "Literary Notices," ibid., 8 October 1874, 6.

62. "Walking," ibid., 5 September 1877, 6; "Literary Notices," ibid., 13 January 1874, 6.

63. "Legs," ibid., 16 November 1874, 2; "Literary Notices," ibid., 16 May 1873, 2; "Literary Notices," ibid., 13 January 1874, 6, *re* Albert H. Hayes' *Diseases of the Nervous System;* "Literary Notices," ibid., 17 October 1874, 6, *re* Dr. E. H. Clarke's *The Building of a Brain.*

64. "The Modern Increase in the Average Life," *Springfield Union,* 4 September 1873, 4.

65. "The Modern Increase in the Average Life"; "The Modern Revival of Muscle," *Springfield Union,* 17 July 1873, 4; "Literary Notices," ibid., 10 July 1875, 6, *re* Dr. Fothergill's *Maintenance of Health.*

66. "Our Prospective Sovereigns," *Nationalist* (July 1889):68–69; Bellamy in interview, "Author of Looking Backward and his Scheme of Nationalization," *Free Press Telegram,* 28 February 18??, clipping in Bellamy family files, Springfield, Mass.; letter of Bellamy, quoted by Cyrus Willard, "News of the Movement," *Nationalist* 1 (3 July 1889):91; Bellamy quoted in "Attitudes of the Press," ibid., 1 (November 1889):273–74; letter of Bellamy read to Cooper Union Conference, quoted in "School Conference Report on the State of the Schools" (New York, 1890), 8.

67. "Should Every Boy Learn a Trade? And How Shall He find Out What He is Best Fitted For?" *New Nation* 2 (2 September 1892):557.

68. Ibid. See also "Too Many College Men Already," ibid. 1 (10 October 1891):583; "Small Help in a Good Education," ibid. 3 (1 April 1893):167–68; "Educated Men Need not Apply," ibid 3 (12 August 1893):387.

69. Folder XXIV, "Woman Worship," 23.

70. Ibid., 9.

71. Bellamy journal possessed by the late Marion Bellamy Earnshaw, Springfield, Mass., n. p.; *Miss Ludington's Sister,* 105; "A Positive Romance," *Blindman's World,* 296, 304–6, 311.

72. Notebook II (187?), 26.

73. *Six to One,* 65, 25.

74. Folder XXX, "A Positive Romance" MS., 4; Folder XXV *re* Bob and Celia.

75. Folder XXXII, "The girl who wished she were a boy . . .," 1–14.

76. "The Escort Question," *Springfield Union,* 14 April 1874, 6.

77. "The Woman's Congress," *Springfield Union,* 17 October 1873, 2; "The Present Status of the 'Woman Movement'," ibid., 15 October 1873, 7.

78. Julia Ward Howe, "Women in the Professions," *Chatauquan* 7 (May 1887):460–62; "Literary Notices," *Springfield Union,* 21 August 1873:6.

79. *Springfield Union,* 21 December 1875, 2.

80. Ibid., 3 February 1877, 6.

81. Ibid., 24 March 1873, 2.

82. "Who Shall Be the City Physician," ibid., 17 January 1873, 2.

83. Notebook XIV, 49; "The New Magazines," *Springfield Union,* 17 November 1877, 4.

84. Frances Willard, "An Interview with Edward Bellamy," *Our Day* 4 (December 1889):540.

85. "The War for Women's Independence Must Become Socialistic," *New Nation* 3 (28 October 1893):474.

86. "The Only Prevention of Prostitution," *New Nation* 1 (28 November 1891):694; "Our Present Social System 'An Agreement with Death and a Covenant with Hell'," ibid. 2 (18 April 1892):241–42; "Why All Women Should Be Nationalists," ibid. 2 (4 June 1892):356; "The Word 'Obey' in the Marriage Ceremony," ibid. 2 (18 June 1892):387.

87. "Talks on Nationalism," *New Nation* 1 (18 April 1891):192.

88. Notebook VII (188?), 20–21; Notebook III (187?), 60–64.

89. "Literary Notices," *Springfield Union,* 22 May 1875, 6.

90. Excerpt from the Bellamy journal in possession of the late Marion Bellamy Earnshaw, n.p.; also, Notebook C (188?), 14; Folder XXXIII, "The Medium's Story," 94; "Pott's Painless Cure," *Blindman's World,* 164.

91. "Literary Notices," *Springfield Union,* 23 September 1876, 6; ibid., 13 November 1872, 2.

92. "Literary Notices," ibid., 6 February 1875, 6, *re* the anonymous *Bazaar Book of the Household,* a collection of essays about domestic life and marriage which advocated that rich not marry the rich. Ibid., 11 April 1873, 2, *re* E. B. Emory in *Queens,* which argued that a Christian woman should not marry a man not one—an idea Bellamy considered "an unmissionary notion" and an "unchristian" one; "A Delicate Question," ibid., 5 August 1875, 4.

93. Notebook IV (187?), 120; Notebook IV (187?), 37; "Literary Notices," *Springfield Union,* 30 January 1873, 6, *re* Katherine S. Macquoid, *My Story,* about a woman who married a man she did not love.

94. "Who Should Not Marry," *Springfield Union,* 20 September 1873, 4.

95. Ibid.; "Stirpiculture," ibid., 2 October 1875, 4.

96. Notebook XIV (187?), 113–16.

97. "A Love Story Reversed," *Blindman's World,* 192–236.

98. "A Brief Summary of the Industrial Plan of Nationalism Set Forth . . . for Class Study," *Dawn* 1 (September 1889), 3; *Looking Backward,* 217–18.

99. "Will the World Be Over-peopled Under Nationalism," *New Nation* 3 (3 February 1894):51; "Talks on Nationalism," ibid. (6 June 1891):298; "The Bogy of Nationalism," ibid. 2 (16 April 1892):242; Notebook VII (189?), 43–44.

100. Ibid.

101. "Literary Notices," *Springfield Union,* 18 February 1874, 6.

102. "The Zone System with a Local Application," *New Nation* 1 (26 September 1891):551.

103. " 'Looking Backward' Again," 359.

104. "Flood Disasters and Nationalism," *New Nation* 2 (1 June 1892):371.

105. [Anon.], "Scientific Intelligence: Paper Window Shutters," *Springfield Union,* 11 January 1873.

106. Ibid., 9 February 1874, 6; "Literary Notices," ibid., 23 September 1876, 6; "Tea Table Talk," *Springfield Daily News,* 14 January 1881, 3.

107. Mrs. E. L. H. W., "Home Correspondence: Women's Press Association and Mr. Bellamy's Service Problem," *Good Housekeeping* 10 (29 March 1890):262.

108. "A Vital Domestic Problem," *Good Housekeeping* 10 (21 December 1889):74–77.

109. "We Accept the Title," *New Nation* 1 (4 July 1891):359.

Chapter Five

1. Cyrus Willard, "The Nationalist Club of Boston," *Nationalist* 1 (May 1889):16.

2. "Declaration of Principles."

3. F. I. Vassault, "Nationalism in California," *Overland Monthly* n.s. 15 (June 1890):660.

4. Cyrus Willard, "A Retrospect," *Nationalist* 2 (December 1889):38–39.

5. Ibid., 38.

6. Green, "Biography," 139.

7. Vassault, "Nationalism in California," 61; J. A. Martin, "A Co-operative Commonwealth," *Nationalist* 1 (October 1889):204–8.

8. Cyrus Willard, "News of the Movement," *Nationalist* 2 (January 1890):75.

9. Cyrus Willard, "A Practical Suggestion for Nationalist Clubs," ibid. (December 1889):56.

10. "Progress of Nationalism in the United States," 751–52.

11. "Nationalism—Principles and Purposes," Address at Tremont Temple, Boston, on the Nationalist Club's First Anniversary, 18 December 1889 (Philadelphia: Bureau of Nationalist Literature, n. d.), 6–10; "Prog-

ress of Nationalism in the United States," 752; "First Steps Toward Nationalism," *Forum* 10 (October 1890):174–84.

12. "The New Party and the Nationalists," *New Nation* 1 (30 May 1891):277–78.

13. "Prospectus," *New Nation* 1 (21 January 1891):13.

14. Ibid.

15. [Anon.], "Third Party in Many States," "A Glance the Country Over," *New Nation* 1 (4 April 1891):149.

16. Green, "Biography," cited by Morgan, *Edward Bellamy,* 278.

17. William Dean Howells, *Literature and Life* (New York, 1902), 294, cited by Elizabeth Sadler, "One Book's Influence," *New England Quarterly* 17 (December 1944):538.

18. C. E. Russell, *Bare Hands and Stone Walls* (New York, Charles Scribner's Sons, 1933), 74–77.

19. "The New Party and the Nationalists," 277–78.

20. Ibid.

21. [Anon.], "The Cradle of Liberty Rocked," *New Nation* 1 (17 October 1891):606–8.

22. [Anon.], "Nationalism in Politics," *New Nation* 2 (22 October 1892):643–45.

23. Green, "Biography," cited by Morgan, *Edward Bellamy,* 282–83.

24. Ibid., 282.

25. [Anon.], "Nationalists in Council," *New Nation* 2 (23 July 1892):469.

26. Letters of B. Franklin Hunter, Philadelphia, to Bellamy, 15 April 1894, 12 May 1894, 3 April 1895, 16 September 1895, 26 October 1897, 23 March 1898.

27. Sadler, "One Book's Influence," 540.

28. Russell, *Bare Hands and Stone Walls,* 74–77.

29. [Anon.], "An Attempt to Fool the Public," *New Nation* 3 (25 November 1893):507.

30. Howard H. Quint, *The Forging of American Socialism* (Columbia, S.C.: University of South Carolina Press, 1953), 112.

31. *Dawn* cited in "Announcement of an Excellent Publication," *New Nation* 1 (18 April 1891):182.

32. Letter of W. D. P. Bliss, to Bellamy, April 1889.

33. "Four Distinctive Principles of Nationalism," *New Nation* 2 (9 January 1892):17–18.

34. Quint, *Forging of . . . Socialism,* 114–15.

35. Ibid., 117.

36. Ibid., 119, 120–122.

37. Ibid., 266–67, 213.

38. Henry Steele Commager, *The American Mind* (New Haven: Yale University Press, 1950), 171, 174.

39. Ibid., 292.

40. Daniel Bell, "Marxian Socialism in the United States" in Donald Drew Egbert and S. Persons, eds., *Socialism and American Life* (Princeton, N.J.: Princeton University Press, 1952), I:264.

41. Ibid., 265–66.

42. Daniel DeLeon, "The Socialist Movement in America," *Weekly People,* 10 October 1959, 2.

43. Bell, "Marxian Socialism," 276. For a detailed account of affairs and controversies, see Quint, *Forging of . . . Socialism,* 350–88.

44. T. W. Higginson, "Step by Step," *Nationalist* 1 (September 1889):145.

45. Green, "Biography," 63.

46. [Anon.], "Edward Bellamy," *Springfield Union,* 1888, Chicopee Falls Library file.

47. Morgan, *Edward Bellamy,* 261.

48. Ibid.

49. Cyrus Willard, unpublished autobiography, chapter 2, 12; Morgan MSS, Houghton Library.

50. Letter of W. Q. Judge, quoted in Morgan, *Edward Bellamy,* 262–63.

51. Letter of Abbott Clark, quoted in Morgan, *Edward Bellamy,* 266–67.

52. Ibid., 275.

53. Letter of Cyrus Field Willard, Chicago, to Bellamy, 3 August 1897.

54. Ibid.

55. Sadler, "One Book's Influence," 547–49.

56. Peter H. Curtis, "Bellamy Nationalism and Later Reform Movements, 1888–1940" (Ph.D. diss.: Indiana University, 1973), 209. See also Sadler, "One Book's Influence," 547–49.

57. Sadler, "One Book's Influence," 548.

58. Upton Sinclair letter to author. See also Sinclair's "A Utopian Bookshelf" *Saturday Review* (7 December 1945), 20 (quoted below).

59. [Anon.], *The Edward Bellamy Association of New York,* published by the Edward Bellamy Association of New York, 7. In Los Angeles in the 1950s and 1960s an association of individuals interested in the ideas of Bellamy published the *Equalitarian Bulletin,* which not only advocated reading *Looking Backward* and *Equality* but contained correspondence from other countries and states.

60. J. H. Franklin, "Edward Bellamy and the Nationalist Movement," *New England Quarterly* 11 (December 1938):739ff.

61. For more details, see Arthur M. Schlesinger, *The Age of Roosevelt: The Politics of Upheaval* (Boston: Houghton Mifflin, 1960), 28–41; David H. Bennett, *Demagogues in the Depression: American Radicals and the Union Party, 1932–36* (New Brunswick, N.J., 153).

62. For more information consult Henry Elsner, Jr., *The Technocrats, Prophets of Automation* (Syracuse, N.Y.: Syracuse University Press, 1967), 46–47, 55, 186–219; Frank P. Stockbridge, "Edward Bellamy, Prophet of Technocracy," *American Press* 51 (January 1933):15–31.

63. Elsner, *Technocrats*, 41.

64. Quotation from Alfred M. Bingham's *Insurgent American* in Schlesinger, *Age of Roosevelt*, 149. Quotations regarding Dewey and Beard are from Bingham's *Common Sense*.

65. Letter of Norman Thomas to author, 29 July 1958.

66. James C. Duram, *Norman Thomas* (New York, 1974), 2.

67. Ibid., 27.

68. Ibid. The quotation is from the recording "Norman Thomas Reminisces," (New Rochelle, N.Y.: Spoken Artis, 1959).

69. Ibid., 83. The quotation is from Norman Thomas, *Socialism Re-examined* (New York, 1963), 209.

70. Letter of Eleanor Roosevelt to author, 28 July 1959.

71. Letter of Irving H. Flamm to author, 24 September 1958.

72. Schlesinger, *Age of Roosevelt*, 365.

73. Arthur Morgan, *Nowhere Was Somewhere* (Chapel Hill: University of North Carolina Press, 1946), 9.

74. Morgan, *Edward Bellamy*, xii.

75. Ibid., 296; MacNair, *Edward Bellamy*, 333–34.

76. Bruno Bettelheim, *The Informed Heart: Autonomy in a Mass Age* (Glencoe, Ill.: Free Press, 1960), 83.

77. Oscar Wilde, *The Soul of Man under Socialism* (Boston: J. W. Luce & Co., 1910), 27.

Selected Bibliography

Only Bellamy's Utopian novels and the published version of his *Religion of Solidarity* are cited in the primary sources here; the first cited edition is the one to which references are made in the text. Bellamy's short stories, his other novels, and his articles and reviews are identified in Notes and References. For more extensive primary bibliographical material, see *The Year 2000: A Critical Biography of Edward Bellamy*, which contains not only articles signed by Bellamy but also his unsigned editorials and reviews in the *Springfield Union;* Everett W. MacNair, *Edward Bellamy and the Nationalist Movement, 1889–1894;* Kenneth M. Roemer, *The Obsolete Necessity: America in Utopian Writing, 1888–1900;* and two bibliographies published in *American Literary Realism,* 1 (Fall, 1967) and 4 (Summer, 1971).

PRIMARY SOURCES

1. Manuscripts
   An extensive collection of Edward Bellamy's manuscripts was discovered in the attic of the home in Chicopee Falls by the late Paul Bellamy and given to Arthur Morgan shortly before his book about Bellamy was completed. Morgan gave this material, as well as items he had collected and some of his correspondence, to the Houghton Library, Harvard University.
   Items cited as in the possession of Marian Bellamy Earnshaw and Mrs. Emma Bellamy were to have been placed in the Bellamy Museum, Chicopee Falls, Massachusetts, after Mrs. Earnshaw's decease.

2. Books
Equality. New York: D. Appleton & Co., 1933. Upper Saddle River, N.J.: Gregg Press, 1968.
Looking Backward. Introduction by Heywood Broun. New York: Modern Library, n. d.
Religion of Solidarity. With a Discussion of Edward Bellamy's Philosophy by Arthur E. Morgan. Yellow Springs, Ohio: Antioch Bookplate Company, Ohio, 1940. Bellamy's work is also reprinted in Arthur E. Morgan, *The Philosophy of Edward Bellamy.* New York: King's Crown Press, 1945.

Talks on Nationalism. Chicago: Peerage Press, 1938. Reprints of "Talks on Nationalism" published in *New Nation.*
Edward Bellamy Speaks Again. Foreword by Lester McBride. Kansas City, Kansas: Peerage Press, 1937.
Edward Bellamy: Selected Writings on Religion and Society. Edited with Introduction by Joseph Schiffman. The American Heritage Series. New York: Liberal Arts Press, 1955. Contains reprint of Morgan's *Religion of Solidarity,* excerpts from *Looking Backward,* and other Bellamy items that express the major themes in Bellamy's writings, such as Journal 7, *Equality,* and *Talks on Nationalism.*

SECONDARY SOURCES

This section identifies only books written about Bellamy or ones that contain significant information about him, Nationalism, or Populism.

Bowman, Sylvia E. *Edward Bellamy Abroad: An American Prophet's Influence.* New York: Twayne, 1962. A study of Bellamy's worldwide effect. Contains an extensive bibliography listing translations of the utopian novels and articles about them.
————*The Year 2000: A Critical Biography of Edward Bellamy.* New York: Bookman Associates, 1958. Reissued: New York: Octagon Books, 1979. Detailed study of Bellamy's life and thought, his editorials, and his book reviews—articles that show parallels with ideas expressed in the utopian novels.
Egbert, Donald Drew, and Persons, Stow, eds. *Socialism and American Life.* 2 vols. Princeton, N.J.: Princeton University Press, 1952. About American socialism and its different developments. Bibliographies in Volume 2 about different groups and settlements.
MacNair, Everett W. *Edward Bellamy and the Nationalist Movement, 1889–1894.* Milwaukee: Fitzgerald Co., 1957. Most useful for identifying groups and individuals who belonged to Bellamy or Nationalist clubs in the United States.
Morgan, Arthur E. *Edward Bellamy.* New York: Columbia University Press, 1944. The first biography of Bellamy. Paved the way for more detailed study of his manuscripts. Contains appraisals of and many quotations from Bellamy's manuscripts.
Quint, Howard H. *The Forging of American Socialism: Origins of the Modern Movement.* Columbia: University of South Carolina Press, 1953. Interesting discussions of Bellamy's socialism, Christian Socialism, and Populism, as well as individuals such as W. D. P. Bliss, Debs, and others.

Roemer, Kenneth. *The Obsolete Necessity: America in Utopian Writings, 1888–1900.* Kent, Ohio: Kent State University Press, 1976. Very interesting study discusses utopian, anti-utopian, and semi-utopian fiction and non-fiction; Bellamy's utopias are frequently used for comparisons and contrasts. As noted earlier, the bibliography is extensive and helpful relative to utopian publications.

Schlesinger, Arthur M., Jr. *The Coming of the New Deal.* Boston: Houghton Mifflin Co., 1959. About Roosevelt and movements of the era, some of which were influenced by Bellamy.

Taylor, Walter Fuller. *The Economic Novel in America.* Chapel Hill: University of North Carolina Press, 1942. Interesting chapters about Bellamy and Howells, a supporter of the *New Nation.* Stresses the cultural heritage of their period.

Index